Government of Michigan
Under the 1964 Constitution

MICHIGAN'S DIVIDED MULTI-LANE HIGHWAYS

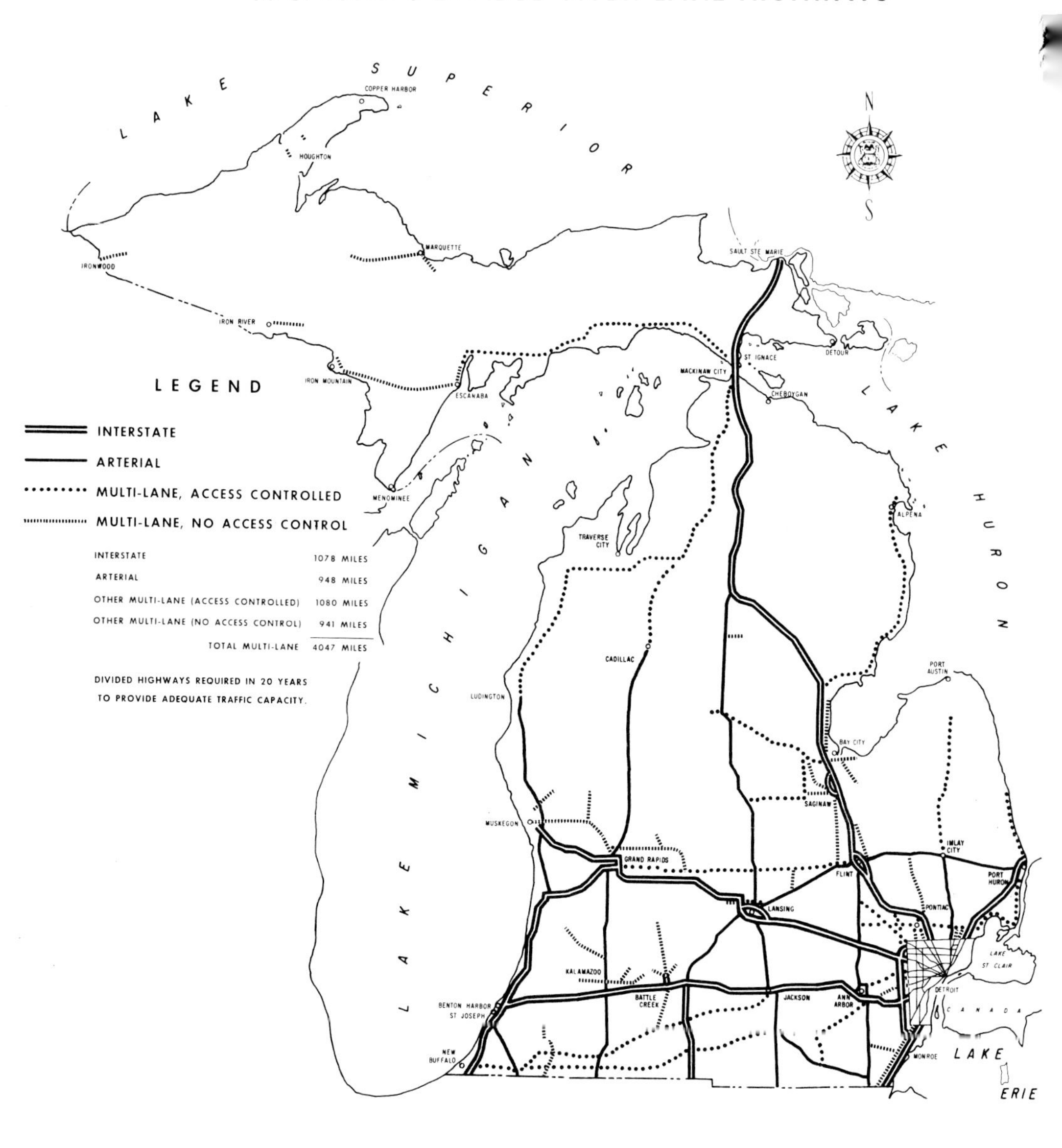

GOVERNMENT OF MICHIGAN

Under the 1964 Constitution

---

by
Robert W. Carr

Ann Arbor
THE UNIVERSITY OF MICHIGAN PRESS

Library of Congress Catalog Card No. 67-14740
Published in the United States of America by
The University of Michigan Press and simultaneously
in Rexdale, Canada, by Ambassador Books Limited
Manufactured in the United States of America

Preface

In April 1963 the voters of Michigan approved a new state constitution. Since then, a number of changes have been made in Michigan's government. The purpose of this book is to describe the basic structure of the state's government as it is established under the new basic law.

The text assumes that the student has some familiarity with government in general, but that he has little specific knowledge of the government of Michigan. The book is intended for use by junior high and senior high students.

The author wishes to express his appreciation to W. Scott Westerman, former coordinator of social studies, Ann Arbor Public Schools, whose encouragement was instrumental in the undertaking of this writing; to Michael J. Berla, LeRoy Cappaert, Barbara M. Carr, and Jean L. King, each of whom read portions of the manuscript and made many helpful suggestions and comments; and to Ferrell Heady, formerly director of the Institute of Public Administration, University of Michigan, for permission to use information concerning the constitutional convention delegates appearing in A. L. Sturm's book cited in the Bibliography. The author assumes sole responsibility for errors, omissions, or misleading statements.

Ann Arbor, Michigan

Contents

Courtesy: Mackinac Bridge Authority

The Mackinac Bridge, linking the Upper and Lower Peninsulas, has become a symbol of Michigan's progress as a state. Construction was started in 1954 and the bridge was opened to the public in November 1957. One of the longest (five miles) suspension bridges in the world, "Mighty Mac" brings Michigan's two peninsulas closer together.

CHAPTER I

MICHIGAN WRITES A BASIC LAW

Constitutions in Michigan

This has been one of the rare privileges of my life to have served with you. As I have said every time I have spoken around the state, I have never been associated with a finer group, a more dedicated group, or one more devoted than you have been. . . .

—Stephen S. Nisbet
president, Michigan Constitutional Convention, during the final moments of the convention.

constitutional convention

On August 1, 1962, at the Civic Center Building in Lansing, 141 men and women assembled. They knew each other well. From October until May they had met together in that building as elected representatives of the people of Michigan. It had been their duty to write a new constitution for the state.

They were the delegates to a Michigan Constitutional Convention.

vote of delegates

Their task was now almost completed. The main job on this day would be whether to give final approval to what they had done. After some discussion of changes, the vote was taken on the motion to pass "the revised constitution as finally amended." Each delegate pressed a button at his desk. On the electric scoreboard at the front of the auditorium the result was clear: 98 for approval and 43 against.* The delegates had approved the constitution; now the

* Three delegates were not present for the official vote of the convention.

people would vote on it. For most citizens this would be the first opportunity to vote on a new constitution for Michigan. The last time the people voted on the constitution was in 1909, and women were not permitted to vote at that time.

Eight months after it had been approved by the delegates the voters of Michigan, by a vote of 810,860 to 803,436, accepted the new document, and on January 1, 1964, the state had a new basic law.

Michigan's constitutions

The constitution of 1964 is Michigan's fourth. The first one was written in 1835 just before Michigan became a state. The others were completed by constitutional conventions held in 1850 and 1907–8. The constitution of 1850 was changed very little by the convention of 1907–8, and so Michigan had practically the same basic law for 113 years, although the 1908 constitution was amended sixty-nine times.

It is interesting to review the major steps which brought about the new constitution of 1964. The effort involved thousands of people working for long hours without pay. There was much debate, discussion, and exchange of ideas. Many Michigan citizens learned more about their state government.

Beginning in the 1940's and 1950's, a number of people in Michigan began to feel that the state needed a new constitution. Why did many citizens feel this way?

objections to the constitution of 1908

For one thing, Michigan was beginning to suffer financially. There were times when it appeared that the state government would be unable to pay its debts. Some people felt that they were being taxed unfairly by the state, while others believed that something had to be done about the tax structure in order to encourage more business growth in Michigan.

Some Michigan residents said that they were not being fairly represented in the legislature, which makes the laws for the state. Others said the governor needed more authority and that new ways needed to be found to enable the governor and the legislature to work together more effectively.

Still other citizens were convinced that the 1908 constitution, written in the "horse and buggy" days, was old-fashioned and that Michigan needed a basic law more suited to the "space age." They said that the state should have a constitution which would be free from details and restrictions on the government and would better allow the state to solve its problems in the decades to come.

And so, enthusiasm grew for calling a constitutional convention.

leaders in convention movement

Many groups combined to lead the movement to call a constitutional convention. Among them were the League of Women Voters of Michigan, the Michigan Junior Chambers of Commerce, and a new group, Citizens for Michigan. They informed and persuaded people, advertised the need for changes in the constitution, and carried petitions necessary for getting on the ballot the various steps needed to call a convention.

steps toward the convention

In November 1960 the voters approved an amendment to the 1908 constitution which, among other things, changed the vote required to call a convention from a majority of those voting *in the election* to a majority of those voting *on the question itself*. It also provided for a vote on calling the convention for April 1961.

In the April election the voters approved calling the constitutional convention by a vote of 596,433 to 573,012. The election of delegates was held the following September. The convention met in Lansing from October 1961 until the following May, officially adjourning on August 1.

who were the delegates?

It is interesting to look at the kinds of people who were delegates to the convention. Of the 144 delegates, eleven were women. There were thirteen Negroes. Politically, the voters elected ninety-nine Republicans and forty-five Democrats. For information concerning the age, education, and income of the delegates, see Figure I.

final vote

The delegates wrote the new state constitution which was accepted by the voters. The League of Women Voters and the Junior Chambers of Commerce were again active, campaigning for a "yes" vote. In addition, the political parties took sides on the issue, with the state Republicans asking for approval and the Michigan Democratic party urging a "no" vote.

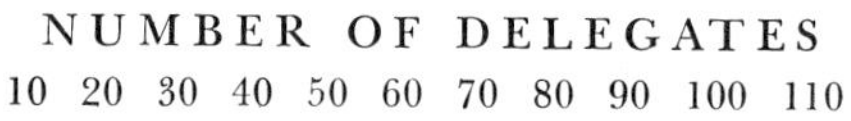

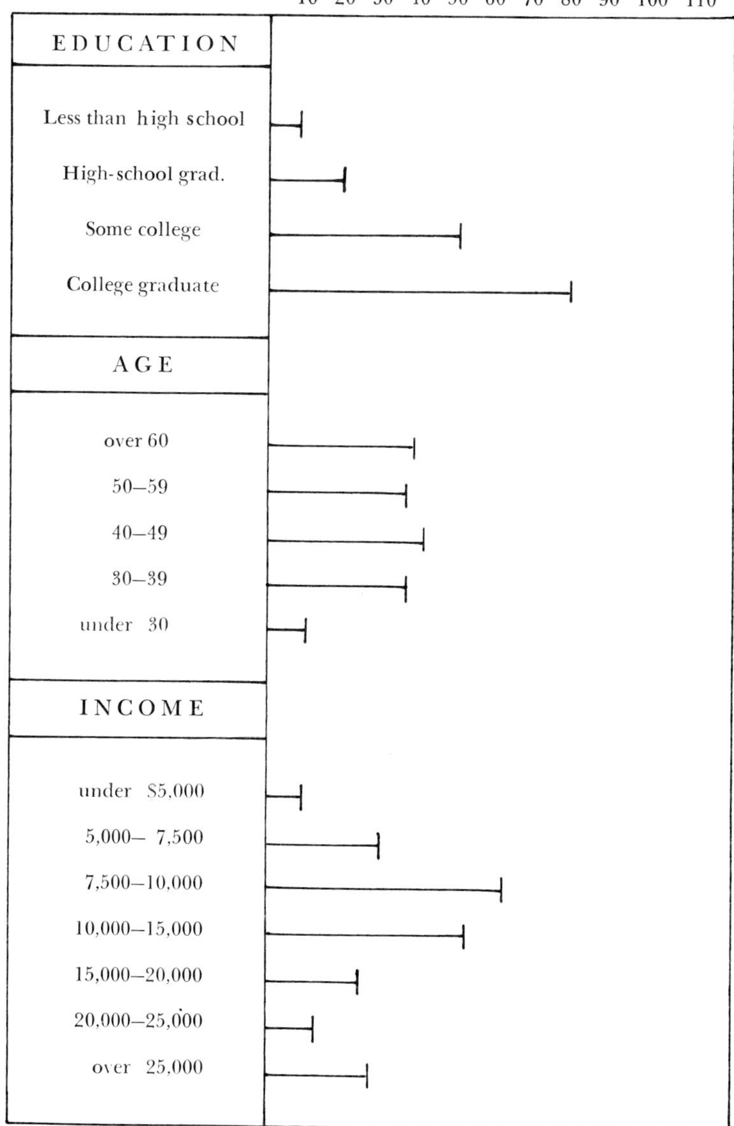

Figure I
Profile of Delegates
Michigan Constitutional Convention, 1961-62.

In this book, we shall become acquainted with the government of Michigan as it now exists under this constitution. You should know about your state's government since its activities affect your daily life in many, many ways.

FOR DISCUSSION AND STUDY

1. Several delegates to the constitutional convention later became candidates for other offices in the government. Can you explain why? List several reasons.

2. As you have read, the League of Women Voters of Michigan was active throughout the campaign for a new constitution. Try to find out more about this energetic, active group of women. Reports would be interesting.

3. In this book you will read about many changes which the 1964 constitution made in Michigan's government. It might be interesting to compare one or two articles of the new constitution with the same parts of the 1908 document. (Your library has a copy of it in the *Michigan Manual* of any year before 1965.) You will see that much of the 1908 constitution was retained, and that some changes were made. This would make an informative project to report on to the class.

CHAPTER II

FREEDOMS AND PROTECTIONS

Individual Rights

> Those who deny freedom to others deserve it not for themselves, and, under a just God, cannot long retain it.
>
> —Abraham Lincoln

"You can't do that; it's against the constitution!"

"This is a free country. I've got my rights!"

"I'll sue you. You can't do that in America and get away with it!"

How often have we heard such remarks! And yet, it is easy to take these statements for granted. What do they really mean?

When most people speak of the "constitution" they are referring to the federal constitution adopted in 1789. But Michigan also has a constitution, as have all the states. Michigan's is one of the new ones in the United States.

The constitution gives "permission" to the state to pass laws, and it prevents other laws from being passed. The specific laws of the state are based on the provisions of the constitution.

The average citizen tends to think that a constitution protects him from unjust acts of the government and gives to him the freedom to speak, to worship, to assemble, and do other things. This is a second purpose of a constitution. How does Michigan's constitution attempt to accomplish this?

Prohibitions on the State

The state constitution makes it clear that there are several things the state may *not* do when dealing with individual citizens.

what states cannot do in dealing with individuals

1. The state may not force anyone to attend, contribute to, any place of religious worship, nor may it reduce a person's civil rights because of his religious beliefs.

2. It may not quarter soldiers in a house in time of peace without the owner's consent. It may not do so in time of war except in a manner prescribed by law.

3. It may not permit slavery.

4. It may not unreasonably search or seize a person, his home, possessions, or papers. Evidence seized during a search may not be used in court unless a warrant previously has been issued, describing the evidence. The exceptions to this are narcotics, firearms, bombs, and other dangerous weapons seized outside a person's home. These may be used as evidence even though they were seized without a warrant.

5. It may not bring a person to trial twice for the same crime.

6. It may not force a person to be a witness against himself.

7. It may not charge excessive fines nor require excessive bail.

8. It may not imprison a person for a debt.

9. It may not deprive a person of life, liberty, or property without due process of law. Private property cannot be taken for a public use without a fair payment. The payment must be determined in a court.

10. It may not convict a person of treason unless he makes war against the state, or helps its enemies, and unless there are two witnesses, or he confesses.

11. It may not require the death penalty.

civil rights commission

12. It may not discriminate against anyone in the exercise of his civil or political rights because of race, color, religion, or national origin. The constitution of of 1964 established a *civil rights commission.* This commission is composed of eight persons, of whom not more than four can be members of the same political party. The members are appointed by the governor with the approval of the senate.

The commission investigates cases in which persons claim that they have suffered discrimination in the exercise of their civil rights due to race, color, religion, or national origin. For example, if a person feels that he has been prevented from voting because of his race, he may take the matter to the commission. In cases in which it finds such discrimination, the commission has the duty to secure the rights of persons discriminated against.

Michigan was the first state to establish a civil rights commission of this kind in its constitution.

Rights

The Michigan constitution also guarantees certain civil and political rights to individuals. These include the rights of all people and those of persons who have been accused of crimes.

rights of all persons

Under the state constitution, all persons enjoy:

1. the right to assemble peaceably;

2. the right to petition the government;

3. freedom of worship;

4. freedom of speech and expression of views, with a responsibility for the abuse of this freedom;

5. the right to keep and bear arms to protect themselves and to defend the state.

When a person has been accused of a crime he has:

1. the right to a speedy, public, and impartial trial by jury;

rights of accused persons

2. the right to defend himself in court and the right to secure a lawyer for his defense;

3. the right to fair and just treatment during investigations by state government;

4. the right to be informed of the crime of which he has been accused, the right to be confronted by the witnesses against him, and the right to get witnesses in his favor;

5. the right to a writ of habeas corpus, which requires the person to be brought before a judge and prevents his being held indefinitely without a trial;

6. the right to appeal a conviction or decision to a higher court.

There is no more important section of a constitution than the one which guarantees individual rights and which protects the citizen from harsh and unjust acts of his government. You will find these provisions in state constitutions and in the federal constitution. They help distinguish a government "of the people" from dictatorships in which the people have few rights or protections.

FOR THOUGHT AND DISCUSSION

1. Read again the exception to the "search and seizure" provision in the Michigan constitution. Do you think this is wise? It would make an interesting debate.

2. Many of the rights guaranteed by the Michigan constitution are also guaranteed in the United States constitution. Why do you think the writers of the state document felt they had to "repeat" these rights?

3. See how many of the rights of accused persons you can recall. Why are we so careful to give so many rights to persons accused of crimes?

4. Make sure you understand such terms as: habeas corpus, bail, petitioning the government, appeal, warrant, discrimination, due process of law, civil rights, and assemble peaceably.

5. What are the arguments in favor of a death penalty in Michigan? What are the reasons given against such a penalty? What is your opinion?

CHAPTER III

INTO THE VOTING BOOTH

Voting and Elections in Michigan

They have such refined and delicate palates
That they can discover no one worthy of their
ballots,
And then when some one terrible gets elected
They say, there, that's what I expected!

—Ogden Nash
Election Day Is a Holiday

Who can vote in Michigan?

Michigan law tries to encourage voting. The qualifications and the procedures for casting a ballot both help to permit voting on a wide scale.

What are the general qualifications for voting in Michigan?

1. The person must be a citizen of the United States. As you know, a person becomes a citizen of the country by birth, by naturalization, or by the naturalization of his parents.

general voting qualifications

2. The person must have been a resident of Michigan for six months before the election. Residence is usually defined as the place where a person sleeps, keeps his personal belongings, and has a regular place of lodging. If a person has more than one residence, the place at which he spends most of the time is considered the residence for voting purposes.

3. The person must be at least twenty-one years old on election day.

4. The person must meet the requirements of residence in his city, village, or township. In Michigan, for many years, this has been thirty days.

These are the qualifications everyone must meet in order to vote. There are also a few special exceptions to be kept in mind.

special exceptions

1. If a person is in jail or if he is mentally incapable of voting, the legislature may prevent him from voting.

2. In elections for President and vice-president of the United States, the legislature may grant the right to vote to citizens who do not meet the residence requirement. This can be done in two situations:

a) When a citizen has not lived in the state for six months.

b) When a citizen has moved from Michigan and has not yet met the residence requirement of the state to which he has moved.

Keep in mind that these last two exceptions apply only to voting for the President and vice-president of the United States. This provision, first included in the 1964 constitution, is designed to let citizens vote for these two national offices regardless of where they live.

3. In two situations only owners of real property (and their husbands or wives) may vote.

a) When a vote is taken to raise the local property tax rate over the constitutional limit for more than five years. If the vote is for a period of five years or less, all voters may cast ballots.

b) When a vote is taken to issue bonds.

Voter registration

Let us ask and answer a few questions about the important act of registering to vote.

1. What is registration?

registration

Registration is placing one's name on the list of qualified voters. When a person registers, he must answer questions about his age, citizenship, and residence to make sure he is eligible to vote.

2. Why is registration necessary?

Registration makes sure that only qualified persons will vote and that they will vote only once. In early days, when the election officials at the polls knew everyone who came to vote, formal registration was not necessary. Three states still do not require registration.

3. How often must one register in Michigan?

permanent registration

Michigan has *permanent registration.* This means that once a citizen registers to vote, he continues to be registered unless he fails to cast a ballot at least once within a specified number of years. In most areas of Michigan, this period is four years, but some larger communities have chosen to make this two years.

4. When can one register?

time for registration

In Michigan a citizen may register with the proper election official during any time up to thirty days prior to an election.

When are elections held in Michigan?

time for elections

Generally speaking, all elections for national, state, county, and township offices are held on the first Tuesday after the first Monday in November in even-numbered years.

Voting may take place in the state at other times for a variety of purposes, among which might be:

voting at other times

1. Election of officials in cities.

2. Election of members of local boards of education.

3. Party primaries to select candidates for United States senator, United States representative, governor, state senator, state representative, judges of the court of appeals, circuit judges, probate judges, various local offices, circuit court commissioners, and justices of the

peace. The last two offices will go out of existence on or before January 1, 1969.

4. Voting on bond issues.

5. Voting on school taxes.

6. Elections to fill vacancies in elective offices.

7. Election of delegates to a constitutional convention.

8. Voting on a proposed constitution.

What are some other important election laws in Michigan?

There are many laws which are designed to keep elections honest. Among the acts connected with elections which are illegal are:

illegal acts

bribing voters,

threatening voters,

accepting bribes,

voting twice or attempting to do so,

publishing false or deceptive information about candidates,

tampering with the voting machines, ballot boxes, or other equipment,

lying about qualifications when registering or voting,

soliciting votes, passing out campaign literature, placing campaign posters or otherwise trying to influence voting within 100 feet of the entrance to the building in which voting is taking place,

preventing people from getting to the polls to vote.

absentee situations

Absentee voting, when the qualified voter sends his ballot in by mail before election day, is common in Michigan. There are four situations in which it is possible to vote by absentee ballot in our state.

1. The voter knows he will be physically unable to get to the polls on election day.

2. The rules of a voter's religion make it impossible for him to vote on election day.

3. The voter is working as a paid election official in another voting district on election day.

4. The voter knows that he will be absent from the election district during the entire time that the polls will be open.

5. The person is seventy years of age or older.

Marking ballots. Although voting by machine is common in many Michigan areas, the election laws contain very specific regulations for marking a paper ballot. The general rule is that the voter must make a cross inside the circle or square next to the candidate's name. When two lines meet, and do not cross, the vote is counted if it is "apparent that the voter intended to make a cross" inside the circle or square.

Should everyone vote?

Every American knows that it is his duty to vote. The right to vote is not enjoyed by millions of people in the world; voting is one act which makes democracy operate; the proper selection of public officials is vital to the American system of representative government.

And yet many of our citizens have poor voting records. For various reasons, some don't register; others forget to go to the polls on election day. It is disappointing to see a large number of our citizens fail to exercise the right to cast a ballot.

"It is just as well that many of these people do not vote," some students of government say. "If they don't think that voting is very important, they will probably not inform themselves about the candidates and the issues. Their votes would then mean very little."

It would be a good thing if more people voted in our elections, but merely voting is not enough. The voter also has the responsibility to inform himself about the qualifi-

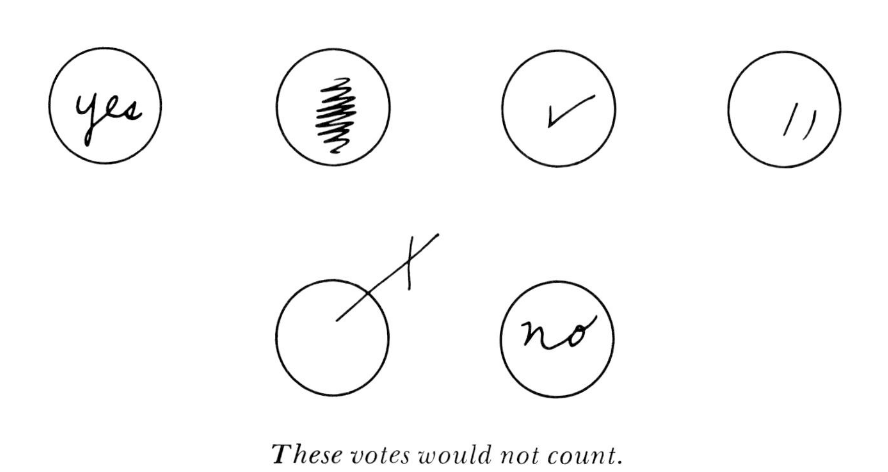

These votes would not count.

These votes would count.

Figure II
Marking Paper Ballots.

cations of the candidates, to discover what the issues are in the election and how the candidates stand on them, and then to vote.

FOR THOUGHT AND DISCUSSION

1. Read again the lines by Ogden Nash quoted at the beginning of the chapter. Write your comments on them.

2. What are some arguments in favor of *requiring* all qualified adults to vote? List also some arguments against the idea.

3. Why do we have a rule against campaigning within 100 feet of the voting place? Describe what might happen if we did not have this rule.

4. "Resolved, that only property owners should be allowed to vote on changes in the property tax." Debate this issue.

CHAPTER IV

LAWMAKERS IN LANSING

Michigan's Legislature

> We have been taught to regard a representative of the people as a sentinel on the watchtower of liberty.
>
> —Daniel Webster

If you visit the capitol when the state legislature is in session, you will have the chance to see democracy at work. Here are the elected representatives of the people of Michigan working on the laws of the state. They are chosen to develop and maintain a set of rules to keep law and order, to preserve rights, and to assure the safety and welfare of the people. They make important decisions which affect our daily lives.

first impression

And yet, you might be disappointed in what you see from your place in the visitors' gallery. Much of what is going on may seem routine. Some legislators might be reading newspapers. Others might be chatting or walking in and out. Many will not be paying attention!

the "routine"

Don't be too concerned. The "routine" is usually the result of long hours of study, debate, and compromise done outside of this chamber. And it is not always routine here! When important and controversial topics are under consideration, the discussion can become quite heated. For lawmaking is serious business, and the effects of a law can be far-reaching indeed.

Let us examine the lawmaking body of Michigan—a body whose actions are so important in our daily lives.

Michigan, like all other states except Nebraska, has a two-house ("bicameral") legislature. We call the houses the "senate" and the "house of representatives." Each house has a large room of its own in the state capitol building.

The house of representatives is a busy, crowded place. There are 110 representatives, each of whom represents roughly 75,000 people. Each representative has a desk which is really his only "office" in Lansing. From the visitors' gallery above this room, one can see the representatives working on letters, talking with other lawmakers, or taking part in the business being carried on.

The senate, on the other side of the capitol building, is much quieter and more relaxed. There are only thirty-eight senators, and the business is usually easier to follow. Each senator represents approximately 220,000 people.

Representatives serve two-year terms and senators serve for four years.

When does the legislature meet?

regular and special sessions

Seventeen states of the Union require their legislatures to meet every year. Michigan has been one of these since 1952. The legislature must meet at twelve o'clock noon on the second Wednesday in January. It may also meet at special times at the request of the governor, and the governor may also require the legislature to meet at another place if meeting at the capitol becomes dangerous for any reason.

Michigan places no limit on the number of days the legislature may meet.

All sessions of the legislature are open to everyone except those which are closed in the interests of public security.

Who can be a legislator?

In order to be a member of either house of the Michigan legislature, a person must:

qualifications for the legislature

1. be a registered voter in the district he represents. He therefore must be twenty-one years old, a citizen of the United States, and he must meet the residence requirements of the city or township in which he lives. If he moves from the district he represents, he is required to resign from office;

2. never have been convicted of subversion;

3. not have been convicted of a felony involving a breach of public trust within twenty years before his election;

4. not be an employee of the United States government, of the state of Michigan, or of any of its political subdivisions. If such a person is elected, he must give up his other government position;

5. not be appointed to any other state office during his term.

In addition, the legislature by a two-thirds vote may expel a member for any reason.

Powers of the legislature

The legislature has the power to pass laws which do not violate the federal or state constitutions, or which do not conflict with powers granted to another branch of the state government.

general powers

Legislators pass laws concerning crime and punishment, taxation, elections, contracts, ownership of property, divorces, marriages, public schools, charitable and penal institutions, libraries, and any matter relating to the health, morals, and welfare of the people of Michigan.

In addition to this general authority, there are various special powers granted to the legislature by the Michigan constitution; among these is the power to:

1. submit bills which have been passed by the legislature to the people for a vote;

2. regulate the use of atomic energy;

specific powers

3. control and supervise state-owned forests and recreational areas and set up state land reserves;

4. set up ports and port districts;

5. establish a liquor control commission to regulate the sale and use of alcoholic beverages;

6. allow a trial by jury of less than twelve persons in civil cases;

7. propose amendments to the state constitution by a two-thirds vote of the members serving in each house —all proposed amendments must be approved by a vote of the people;

8. establish succession to the governorship and other public offices in times of enemy attack when the office-holders and their legal successors are unable to serve.

Limits on the legislature

federal limitations

The federal constitution lists several things which the states are not allowed to do; for example, they cannot coin money, grant titles of nobility, enter into treaties, or deny persons the right to vote on the basis of race, creed, color, or sex. In addition, no state may, without the consent of Congress, keep troops, enter into agreements with other states or foreign countries, or engage in war.

Michigan's legislature is prohibited by the Michigan constitution from interfering with rights of individuals (see Chapter II). The constitution also limits the legislature in the following ways:

1. Neither house may adjourn for more than two days without the permission of the other house.

2. No law can be passed which covers more than one subject.

specific state limitations

3. No bill can be changed on its passage through either house so that its original purpose is altered.

4. If a majority of the voters in a county prohibits the sale or manufacture of alcoholic beverages within the county, neither can be permitted by the legislature.

5. The legislature cannot authorize any lottery.

6. No law providing for the death penalty can be passed.

Forest fires take their toll each year in Michigan. The state government, through the department of conservation, attempts to prevent such disasters. The state legislature must appropriate money each year for the control and prevention of damage to our natural resources.

Courtesy: Michigan Department of Conservation

Duties of the legislature

It is assumed that the legislature will pass laws necessary for the operation of the state and its government. There are, moreover, a number of specific actions that the legislature is required to take. It must, for example, pass laws for the promotion of public health and for the protection of natural resources.

specific duties

The legislators are also required to appoint a state auditor general. His job is to see that the money of the state is being spent properly, to make sure that proper methods are being used to keep track of funds, and to determine whether there is anything improper about the way the state's money is being handled.

the auditor general

The auditor general is appointed for an eight-year term and may be removed from office by a vote of two-thirds of the members of each house. He is required to make an annual report on his work to the legislature and to the governor.

Privileges and immunities of state legislators

Senators and representatives may not be arrested for civil suits and are immune to civil procedures. This immunity applies during, as well as for five days before and five days after, each session of the legislature. It does not apply to criminal charges. No legislator can be questioned anywhere for anything he says in either house.

Naturally, citizens expect that persons serving in public office will exercise self-control and restraint in what they say and do.

How are our legislators paid?

Our legislators set their own salaries. Changes in salary can only take effect at the beginning of the term of the legislators.

salaries

Michigan ranks high among the states in amount of salary paid to legislators. Most Michigan legislators add to this income with money earned from other occupations. In a recent state senate, for example, there were ten attorneys, three men in the real estate business, two labor union officials, three farmers, one funeral director, and one department store president, among others. The house of representatives had ten attorneys and eighteen farmers.

How are laws made by the legislature?

Lawmaking is not an easy or quick process, for it is important to allow time to consider proposals carefully and to hear arguments about the law.

All laws begin as "bills" introduced by one or more members of the legislature. Ideas for bills come from many sources. Let us list a few:

sources of ideas for bills

1. the governor and other state officials;
2. the legislators themselves;
3. various groups (civic, educational, religious, etc.) interested in certain kinds of laws;
4. individual citizens;
5. economic groups—businesses, labor unions, etc.;
6. the "initiative," by which groups of citizens petition for laws.

Let us follow a bill through the legislature.

Bills may be introduced in either house, but let us suppose that this one begins in the senate. The bill is introduced by having its title and purpose read twice. It is then referred to a committee. In the senate there are various committees composed of legislators assigned to work on certain kinds of bills. Lawmakers are appointed to committees by a "committee on committees," whose appointments are approved by the members of the senate. The chairman of each committee is almost always a member of the political party with the most members in the senate. The committees in the senate are:

senate committees

Agriculture
Appropriations
Conservation
Corporations
Education
Elections
Health and Welfare
Highways

Insurance
Interstate Cooperation
Judiciary
Labor
Liquor Control
Municipalities
Public Utilities
Retirement
Senate Business
State Affairs
Taxation
Veterans' Affairs

The committees have a very important job. Committee members listen to arguments, hold hearings to get different points of view, discuss possible changes, and make recommendations about the passage of bills. Hundreds of bills are introduced in the legislature each year. Some eventually become law, but many are not "reported out" of committee and die. Some are not even discussed by the committee.

If the senate committee, in our example, feels that the bill is a good one, the committee will report it back favorably to the senate.

debate and vote

The bill is then debated on the floor of the senate. After debate, the bill's title and subject are read for the third time and the bill may be amended. Then a vote is taken on the bill. Approximately half of the states, including Michigan, provide their legislatures with electrical voting equipment which eliminates the need for time-consuming roll calls. If the bill receives the votes of a majority of the members serving in the senate, it is passed to the house of representatives.

influences on the legislator

How does a legislator decide how to vote on a bill?

1. His general outlook on government. A legislator's vote will be partly determined by how he feels about the part government should play in society.

2. His study and experience. If he has studied the bill, or is experienced with the subject matter of the bill, he will vote accordingly.

3. His party's stand. If the legislator's party has adopted a position about the proposal, this position will influence the lawmaker.

4. The feeling of the people in the district he represents. If the lawmaker gets letters, phone calls, and

telegrams concerning a proposal, his vote may reflect the opinions he hears. He also discovers the views of the people in his district by face-to-face conversation and by reading newspapers in the area. What will the people back home think? Will his vote help him get reelected?

5. Arguments of pressure groups. "Lobbyists" representing all sorts of groups will try to persuade a lawmaker to vote one way or another.

6. Agreements with other legislators. Often bargains are reached in which two or more lawmakers agree to vote on each other's bills.

action in the house

The house of representatives follows the same general procedure as the senate. There are almost fifty committees in the house. In addition to committees which have the same name as those in the senate, the house has committees on such subjects as aeronautics, fish and fisheries, juvenile corrections, metropolitan affairs, social aid and welfare, and ways and means. Some committees in the house of representatives are very busy; some scarcely ever meet. The speaker, or presiding officer, of the house appoints house members to committees.

house committees

If the house of representatives passes the bill, it usually is different from the one passed by the senate. A *conference committee,* made up of both senators and representatives, then attempts to work out a compromise between the two versions. If such a bill is agreed upon, it is sent to the governor.

Upon receiving the bill, the governor must choose among four actions.

1. He can sign the bill. This makes it a law, effective in ninety days. This bill will take effect immediately only if this is agreed to by a two-thirds vote of the members of each house.

choices of action of the governor

2. He can disapprove, or veto, the bill. In that event, he returns it to the house which started it, listing his objections to the bill. This must be done within fourteen days. The legislature may then pass the bill into

law without the governor's signature by a vote of two-thirds of the members serving in each house. This is often called "overriding the governor's veto."

3. The governor may do nothing, and the bill becomes law without his signature after fourteen days, if the legislature is still in session after that time. The governor may choose not to sign the bill because (1) he does not completely agree with its purpose, (2) he knows that his veto would be overridden, or (3) he feels that signing or vetoing the bill would hurt him in the eyes of the voters.

4. If he does nothing, and during the fourteen days the legislature ends its session, the bill does not become law. This is often called the "pocket veto."

legislative council

Our legislators often need help in getting information about laws, in writing bills, and in other ways. To assist lawmakers there is a legislative council, made up of legislators of each political party. The council also examines state laws and recommends changes when necessary.

Legislative apportionment

During the convention of 1961–62 and in the months before the final vote by the people on the new constitution, more debate was centered on the topic of apportionment of the state legislature than on any other single subject.

definition

The term "apportionment" means the manner in which the districts for senators and representatives are drawn, how many citizens each legislator represents, and with how much land area he must concern himself. In order to remain efficient, the legislature is limited to 110 representatives and 38 senators.

To provide equivalent representation the land of the state must be divided into "portions" as fairly as possible. The portions of the state are the districts; one district for each of the representatives, and one for each of the senators.

Why was this such an important debate at the constitutional convention?

importance of apportionment

To understand this, we must remember that the legislators pass the laws as representatives of the people. If some people feel that they are not as well represented as others in the legislature, they might try to establish a new apportionment plan.

Let us use an example to illustrate.

Representative Jones is elected in a district which has a population of 40,000 people, while Representative Smith has 80,000 people in his district. The people living in Smith's district will probably feel that they are not as well represented as those in Jones's district. Smith's people might suspect that they would be less successful in getting the laws they want since their points of view might not be as well expressed in the legislature.

But what if Jones's district is twice as large as Smith's? Is this enough to make up for the difference in population? Or, in these days of fast and easy travel, should area count at all? People in rural areas feel that it should; city dwellers are less likely to think so. Across the nation in recent years, various citizens have gone to court with legal suits asking that the apportionment system in their state be changed. Generally, these are people who feel that they are not as well represented as others in their state legislature.

"area" and "population"

The problem of forming the districts is not an easy one. One needs to decide, for example, on the importance of the "area" factor, how equal the population of the districts ought to be, who draws the boundaries of the districts, how often they should be drawn, and the like.

Now let us see how the Michigan constitution provides for the apportioning of the legislature.

Apportionment for the senate

In effect, the apportioning of the senate follows the idea that "population" is four times as important as "area."

senate apportionment formula

A system of apportionment "factors" is used. Each county gets factors according to (1) its percentage of the state's population multiplied by four, plus (2) its percentage of the state's land area. In order to qualify for a senator, a county must have thirteen factors.

Placing this system in a formula, we see that

county's percentage of population × 4	......
plus county's percentage of land area	......
Total apportionment factors	......

Each county having thirteen or more factors is entitled to one senator. If a county has fewer than thirteen, it is combined with enough neighboring counties so that a district is formed which has no fewer than ten factors and no more than sixteen. Every district must have as close to thirteen factors as possible.

If a county has enough apportionment factors to entitle it to more than one senator, the county is divided into as many districts as there are senators. The districts within the county must be as nearly equal in population as possible.

Assuming that the population of Michigan is 7,820,000, and that the land area is 57,022 square miles, let us take a few examples:

1. County X has a population of 234,600 and an area of 570 square miles. It contains, therefore, 3 percent of the state's population and 1 percent of its land area. Then:

3 percent of population × 4	= 12
plus 1 percent of area	= 1
apportionment factors	13

   County X is entitled to one senator.

2. County Z has a population of 2,521,950 and an area of 570 square miles. It contains, therefore, 32¼ percent of the state's population and 1 percent of its land area. Then:

percent of population × 4	= 129
percent of land area	= 1
apportionment factors	130

   Since a county is entitled to one senator for every thirteen apportionment factors, county Z qualified for ten senators. The county will be be divided into ten districts as nearly equal to each other in population as possible.

Apportionment for the house of representatives

In the house of representatives the apportioning of legislative districts is done on a "population" basis without specifically taking area into account. Each county is entitled to one representative if it contains at least seven-tenths of 1 percent of the state's population.

After each census, the districts are drawn on the basis of the formula

house apportionment formula

$$\frac{\text{State population}}{100} \times \frac{7}{10} = X.$$

Each county which has a population at least as large as X is then given one representative.

Those counties which do not meet this requirement are combined with enough neighboring counties so that the district formed is at least as large as seven-tenths of 1 percent of the population.*

After each county or district is granted one representative, the remaining representatives are apportioned among the counties by the method of "equal proportions." This is a mathematical way of determining which counties should get the additional legislative seats remaining, and how many of them.

As a result, some counties are entitled to more than one representative. These counties are then divided into districts, each of which is represented by a single legislator. The populations of these districts must be as nearly equal as possible, and the districts must follow city and township lines when they are drawn. They also must be as square as possible.

* If there are counties which do not meet the seven-tenths requirement and do not have neighboring counties which need them to meet that requirement, then they are placed in the neighboring districts with the smallest populations.

An example will help to clarify this important, but somewhat complicated, procedure.

Let us assume that the population of Michigan in a given year is 7,820,000. Let us also assume five counties have populations as follows:

County A:	54,750
County B:	2,666,620
County C:	698,160
County D:	406,640
County E:	35,000

The problem is to determine how many legislators each county is entitled to and which ones ought to be assigned additional representatives.

The first step is to determine the minimum requirement for each district. We use the formula and discover that

$$\frac{7{,}820{,}000}{100} \times \frac{7}{10} = 54{,}740$$

Therefore, counties A, B, C, and D will qualify for a seat in the house of representatives, since each has a population larger than the minimum required. County E, it is clear, does not meet the requirement and must be combined with another county or group of counties to form a representative district.

The reapportionment commission then has the job of determining how many additional seats are to be assigned counties such as A, B, C, and D. This is done by assigning additional representatives to each county equal to the percentage of the state population in each county. County B would be assigned thirty-three additional seats in the house of representatives. County A would clearly not qualify for additional legislators since it contains only ten additional residents. Counties C and D would be assigned legislative seats on the basis of their percentage of the state's population.

Naturally, the populations of counties do not exactly equal percentages of the population. The commission compares relative percentages of populations left over and decides on that basis which counties deserve to have the remaining seats in the house of representatives.

Changes in apportionment

recent court decisions

Soon after the 1964 constitution was written, the United States Supreme Court changed the apportionment picture completely. The court ruled that a state may *not* use "area" as a factor in establishing legislative districts. So, Michigan was required to draw new districts which used "population" as the *only* factor. In the 1964 and 1966 elections, state legislators were chosen from these districts.

How do we plan for changes in population?

population shifts

People are constantly moving. Jobs are changed, new work must be found, older people retire, and for a host of other reasons our population is constantly shifting from one place to another. Open farmland is changed to bustling suburbs within a few short years.

This means that some counties in Michigan are gaining population at a faster rate, some are gaining at a slower rate, and some counties are losing population. The districts we draw now will need to be changed in the future so that the counties which grow at a faster rate will be given more legislators.

Let us look at some specific examples in Michigan. Oakland County in 1950 had a population of 396,001. Ten years later its population had risen 74 percent, to 690,583. It obviously is entitled to more representation in both the house of representatives and the senate. The same can be said about Macomb County, whose population during the same period rose from 184,961 to 405,804, or a startling 119 percent.

On the other hand seventeen counties in the state lost population during this period. Houghton County, for example, dropped from 39,771 in 1950 to 35,654 in 1960.

There needs to be some fair method for arranging the legislative districts to adjust to changes in population. The commission on legislative reapportionment is designed to meet this need. The job of this commission is to draw districts every ten years according to the rules we have just described.

reapportionment commission

The reapportionment commission has eight members, four of whom are selected by each major party. If a candidate from a third political party receives more than 25 percent of the total vote at the last election, then that party is allowed to place four persons on the commission.

The four members selected by each party must be registered voters. They must be selected from different parts of the state—one from the Upper Peninsula, one from the northern half of the Lower Peninsula, one from the southwestern part, and one from the southeastern part of Michigan.

If a majority of the commission's members cannot agree on a plan within six months, the individual members may submit plans for apportionment to the supreme court, which then decides which plan follows the constitution most closely.

In 1965 the commission was unable to agree upon an apportionment plan, and the matter was decided by the state supreme court.

The citizen and the legislature

Much of the success of the legislature depends on the interest of the people of the state. This interest can take two major forms. A citizen can help by:

1. encouraging well-qualified persons to run for the legislature and helping them to get elected;

2. taking an interest in bills under discussion in the legislature and expressing his opinions on them.

The service which the state legislature renders the citizen is great. It is impossible to exaggerate the importance of the work of the state senators and representatives. They deserve the support, encouragement, and interest of all.

FOR THOUGHT AND DISCUSSION

1. How do you feel about the requirements for eligibility for the legislature? Would you add, or take away, any of them? Explain.

2. Why are legislators free from civil arrest during sessions of the legislature? Why can they not be held responsible for what they say during meetings of the legislature?

3. What are lobbyists? Do you think they should be regulated by the state government? What kinds of lobbyists would you find in Lansing? Explain.

4. How do you feel about the use of the "area" factor in determining the senate districts? Why do some people feel it must be included? Why do others think it should not be used?

5. Determine the number of senators and representatives to which your county is entitled. Who represents you in each house? Make a report on the background of your state senator or representative.

6. Read the minutes of the constitutional convention during the debate on apportionment of the legislature. Report to the class on the various points of view expressed.

CHAPTER V

LED BY THE GOVERNOR
The Executive Branch

Public officers are the servants of the people, to execute laws which the people have made.

—Grover Cleveland

The governor

the chief executive

The one official in Lansing whom most people "know" is the governor. He is the person the voters hold responsible for the way the state is being run. As former Governor G. Mennen Williams has said,

> "The governor is first of all the servant of the public. Everyone knows him; everyone looks to him for help." *

Let us now look at this prominent office to determine why it has this great importance.

What are the duties of the governor?

As chief executive of the state, the governor has many duties affecting all functions of the state government. Here is a list of some of his most important responsibilities.

1. He supervises the executive branch of Michigan's government, seeing to it that the laws of the state are faithfully carried out.

* Quoted from *A Governor's Notes* by G. Mennen Williams (The University of Michigan Institute of Public Administration), page 4.

duties of the governor

2. He appoints heads of principal departments in the executive branch. Many of these appointments require the approval of the senate, and the senate must act within sixty days of the announcement of the appointment, or it stands approved.

3. He keeps watch on the operation of the other executive offices and on the public officials responsible for them.

4. He makes appointments to fill vacancies in the executive department.

5. He is the commander-in-chief of the armed forces of the state.

6. He reports each year to the legislature concerning the general condition of the state.

7. He submits a budget for the coming year, showing proposed spending and estimated revenues for the year.

8. He prepares bills for the raising of money for the year.

9. He reduces the amount of money spent when it appears that the money being received for a certain state activity is not as great as was originally expected when the budget was prepared.

10. He signs into law bills of which he approves.

11. He informs the legislature of each reprieve, pardon, and commutation made during the year. A reprieve is a temporary suspension of a penalty; a pardon is a release from all penalties; a commutation is a change in punishment to one lesser in degree than the person originally received.

12. He is expected to be the "ceremonial head" of the state, and to appear at special celebrations, festivals, visits of important people, openings of roads and other public works, and a variety of other events.

13. He is a political leader, and the members of his

party expect him to make political appearances and speeches from time to time.

14. He is expected to suggest new laws and to provide leadership in getting important bills passed by the legislature.

What powers does the governor have?

In addition to the duties which the governor has, there are many things that he *may* do when he feels they are necessary or advisable.

powers of the governor

1. He may remove an official from office for a number of reasons, such as

a) neglect of duty,

b) corrupt conduct in office,

c) overstepping legal authority,

d) improper exercise of authority.

2. He may call the legislature into special session to consider only the subjects which he selects. This is usually done in special cases when it seems unwise to wait until the next regular session of the legislature, or when the governor wishes the lawmakers to concentrate on one or two important subjects.

3. He may "veto" any bill of which he does not approve.

4. He may veto any item in an appropriation bill.

5. He may require information from any state official about any subject related to the duties of the official.

6. He may grant reprieves, pardons, and commutations after a person has been found guilty of a crime.

Who can be governor?

qualifications for governor

There are only two formal qualifications for the chief executive of Michigan. First, he must be at least thirty years old. Second, he must have been a registered voter in Michigan for four years immediately preceding his election.

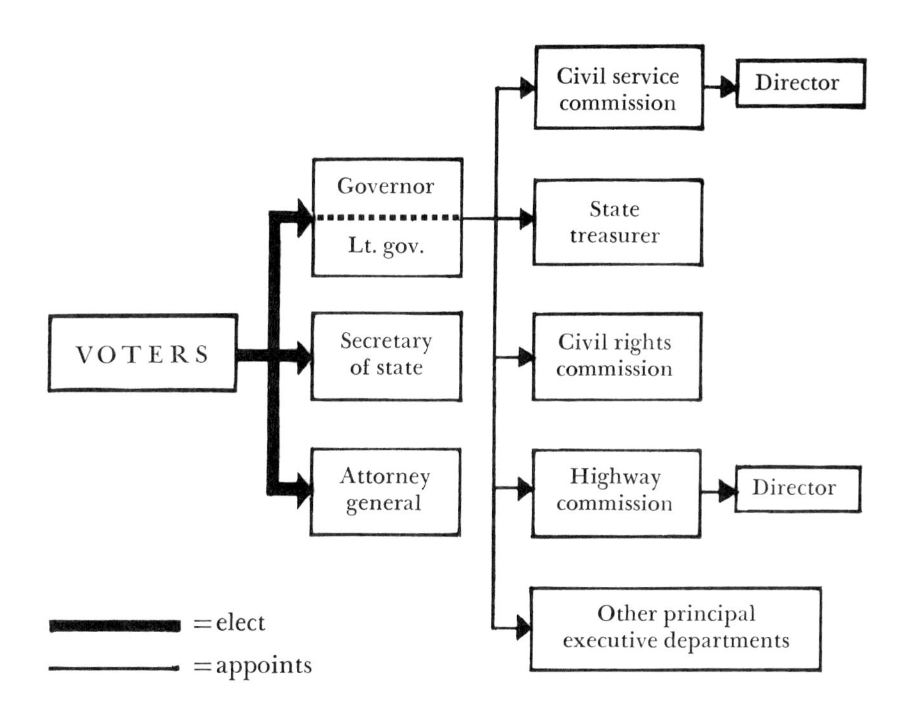

Figure III
The Michigan executive branch.

The second requirement, of course, means that he must meet the voter qualifications of citizenship and residence.

How is the governor elected?

nomination

Candidates for governor of Michigan are chosen, or nominated, in a direct primary held in the state on the first Tuesday following the first Monday in August preceding every general election. The candidate in each party receiving the most votes then runs for governor in the fall election.

The governor serves a four-year term. (Before 1964 the term was two years.) Elections for governor are held at times when an election for United States President is not being held. It seems better to hold these two important elections in different years, so that the voter can concentrate on one at a time.

There is no limit to the number of terms the governor may serve. Three Michigan governors have served all, or part, of at least three terms. The most recent of these was Governor Williams, who served six terms from 1949 to 1961.

election as a team

The governor and the lieutenant governor are elected "as a team." This means that one vote is cast for both candidates of the same party, in the same way that, in national elections, the voter casts one vote for the President and vice-president together. Can you think why it is felt more desirable to elect the governor and the lieutenant governor as a team?

The "team" which receives the most votes is elected and takes office at the beginning of the following year.

A residence for the governor

constitutional provision

The constitution of 1964 provides that the governor be supplied with a suitable place to live, called the governor's residence. Michigan had been one of nine states which did not provide such a place.

Among the reasons given for providing a residence had been:

1. The governor should not be forced to waste valuable time searching for a place to live.

arguments for a residence

2. The governor should not be required to buy and maintain a home in Lansing as well as one in his home town.

3. There needs to be a place where the governor can carry out his social and entertainment responsibilities. Some governors have complained about the lack of a suitable place to entertain distinguished visitors to the state.

4. A residence would serve as a place where the governor and the legislators might meet informally and discuss state affairs.

Succession to the governorship

The elected governor might leave office for a number of reasons.

1. He might die.

causes of vacancy

2. He might resign.

3. He might be impeached and convicted.

4. He might be removed from office in a case of "inability."

impeachment

The governor may be impeached, that is, brought to trial, for corrupt conduct in office or for the committing of a crime. A majority of the members serving in the house of representatives must vote for the impeachment.

trial

Impeachments of the governor are tried by the senate, with the chief justice of the state supreme court presiding at the trial. The governor is removed when two-thirds of the members serving in the senate vote for it.

removal

It may also be that, for some reason, the governor is unable to serve. For example, he may be physically or mentally ill. The speaker of the house of representatives and the president "pro tempore" of the senate, acting together, may ask the supreme court to determine whether the governor is able to continue to remain in office. If a majority of the supreme court justices decides that the governor is not able to serve, he is removed from office. If, later, the supreme court decides that the governor is once again able to serve, he will be restored to office.

succession

If the governor leaves office for any reason, the lieutenant governor becomes the governor. He assumes all the powers, duties, and privileges of the office, including the salary. Following the lieutenant governor in order of succession are the secretary of state, the attorney general, and other state officials.

Other major executive officials

Let us look now at the other officials who carry out the laws of the state in the executive department.

other elected officials

In addition to the governor, there are three officials in the executive branch of state government who are elected by the people directly. They are the lieutenant governor, the secretary of state, and the attorney general. These officials are elected at the same time and serve the same term as the governor. They are nominated at political party state conventions rather than by the direct primary method.

By the time the state conventions are held, the candidates for governor have been chosen in the primary. These persons, if they wish, can have a great influence on whom the convention selects as candidates for the other three elected offices.

Let us now briefly look at these three officials of our state government to learn the nature of their duties and powers.

The lieutenant governor

The qualifications for the lieutenant governor of Michigan are the same as those for governor.

As we have seen, the lieutenant governor becomes the governor when the governor dies, resigns, or is removed from office. He acts as governor when the governor is out of the state.

The lieutenant governor presides at meetings of the senate. He has no vote unless there is a tie in the voting among the senators. The lieutenant governor then may cast the deciding vote.

duties

In addition, the lieutenant governor may perform any duties requested by the governor, except those powers and duties which are specifically given to the governor only.

The secretary of state

For many citizens, the most frequent direct contact with the government of Michigan comes through the office of the secretary of state. When a citizen gets his driver's license, buys license plates for his car, registers to vote, runs for public office, sells his car, or is in need of a record of a business transaction, he deals with this office.

The secretary of state:

1. keeps all records of the state government;

2. establishes rules for the conduct of all elections in the state;

services of the secretary of state

3. registers automobiles and other motor vehicles;

4. issues driver's licenses;

5. issues licenses for detectives;

6. registers trade marks, lobbyists, mortgages, and city and village charters;

7. regulates and supervises savings and loan associations.

The secretary of state currently maintains 228 branch offices in cities and towns throughout the state to serve citizens.

The attorney general

The attorney general is the chief law enforcement officer of the state. He is the lawyer for the legislature and for each state executive officer, as well as for each department, board, and commission of the state government.

While one state police detective photographs the scene around a broken safe as the thieves left it, another officer dusts a file cabinet drawer in an effort to obtain latent fingerprints which may have been made by one of the criminals. Fragments of glass, paint, fiber, along with tool markings, fingerprints, and footprints, are examples of clues which can help officers solve criminal cases.

Courtesy: Michigan State Police

After engaging in a water accident search, state police underwater recovery squad divers come aboard one of two amphibious trucks the department operates. The trucks are used as mobile, floating diver bases, particularly on large bodies of water and when weather conditions would jeopardize the safety of smaller rescue craft.

The identification section at East Lansing state police headquarters receives an average of about 12,000 sets of fingerprints a month, both criminal and noncriminal. The section has more than *five million* sets of prints on file, of which more than half are criminal. Services of the section are available to and used by other enforcement agencies without charge.

Courtesy: Michigan State Police

State police patrols lend a willing hand to drivers stranded by motor or other trouble on Michigan's freeways and other highways. For those in need, troopers arrange for an emergency gas supply and for tows if necessary, assist motorists who become ill, and perform similar services. Troopers assist on the average about 5000 motorists a month.

Some of the duties and powers of the attorney general are as follows:

1. He represents the state, as its lawyer, in all legal matters.

2. He gives advice to prosecuting attorneys in counties throughout Michigan.

the state's lawyer

3. He may enter any case in the state courts when, in his judgment, it is necessary to protect the rights or interests of the state or its people.

4. He gives legal "opinions" when they are requested by the legislature, state officers, departments, boards, or commissions. The attorney general tells what he thinks the laws mean, whether a certain law conflicts with another law, whether it seems constitutional, and the like. These opinions are not binding laws and can be overturned by state courts.

5. He may request that grand juries be established to investigate crime, complaints about public officials, or possible election frauds.

The attorney general maintains a large staff of lawyers to assist him. He appoints a deputy attorney general who has the powers and duties of the office, when the attorney general is absent.

The Michigan constitution requires that two other major departments be established—the department of the state treasurer and the highway department.

The state treasurer

Handling the financial affairs of a state of Michigan's size is a huge task. For example:

money handling

1. The state treasurer receives and deposits in banks all the money for the various branches of Michigan's government. Over two hundred bank accounts are maintained by the state treasurer, and in a recent year the total money deposited was almost $31,000,000.

2. Each month he must account to the auditor general and the superintendent of public instruction for all

money received, spent, and remaining on hand. In an average month, the state treasurer's office writes over 300,000 checks to pay the many costs of the state government.

3. The state treasurer must be prepared to inform the legislature about the current financial operations of the state.

4. He uses surplus funds to purchase United States government securities or other investments. He may invest funds, for example, to provide retirement or pension benefits for public officials and other employees. In a recent year the invested funds of the state earned over $14,700,000 *in interest!*

5. He guards securities deposited with the state by banks, insurance companies, and others.

6. He maintains all the financial records for the state.

7. The state treasurer is the financial agent for bond issues dedicated to superhighways in the state, such as the Detroit-Toledo, Grand Haven-Muskegon, John C. Lodge-Edsel Ford, and the Midland-Bay City expressways. As financial agent, he maintains records, receives and pays out all money, and invests funds not immediately needed.

The state treasurer is appointed by the governor with the consent of the senate and may be discharged by the governor.

The highway commission

roads

In these days of increased travel, Michigan's highway system has become more important than ever before. The completion of the Mackinac Bridge and the rapid development of a network of expressways in the state have reduced greatly the time required for a journey from Detroit to Ironwood.

highway commission

The state highway commission is responsible for the roads in Michigan. The commission is composed of four members, not more than two of whom can be of the same political party. They are appointed by the governor with the consent of the senate.

A member of the highway commission serves four years, and the terms are so arranged that no more than two will end in the same year.

director

The highway commission must appoint a state *highway director* to carry out its policies. The director must be a highway engineer and a competent administrator. The commission may remove the director at any time.

Organization of the executive branch

reorganizing the executive branch

The constitution of 1964 requires that all boards, commissions, and agencies in the executive branch of state government be combined into no more than twenty principal departments.

A listing of a few of the boards, agencies, and commissions existing in 1963 will show how much this reorganization was needed, and how difficult the job of grouping them was. In all there were over 120 executive agencies, such as:

Commission on aging

State safety commission

Agricultural marketing council

Department of aeronautics

Department of agriculture

Department of conservation

Department of corrections

Health department

Insurance commission

Mental health department

Social welfare commission

Veterans' trust fund

Workmen's compensation department

State plumbing board

Board of alcoholism

Athletic board of control

Board of examiners of barbers

State bridge commission

Michigan cherry commission

Civil defense

Civil service commission

Corporation and securities commission

State board of cosmetology

Electrical administrative board

Great Lakes commission

State fair commission

Board of managers of Upper Peninsula state fair

In 1965 the legislature passed a law which reorganized the executive branch. The organization chart shows how this was done under the law.

How are executive officials paid?

salaries

The legislature sets the salaries of Michigan's executive officials. An official's salary may not be changed during his term of office.

other states

Compared with other states, these salaries are fairly high. Five states (California, Illinois, New Jersey, New York, and Pennsylvania) pay their governors more than does Michigan. The average salary paid to the governors of the thirteen best-paying states is slightly more than the salary of Michigan's chief executive.

If we were to compare these salaries with those paid to officials with equal responsibilities in private businesses, they would seem quite low.

Civil service

membership

For over twenty years most of the people who work for the state of Michigan have been employed under a system of "civil service." This system hires, promotes, and pays employees on the basis of their performance, training, and

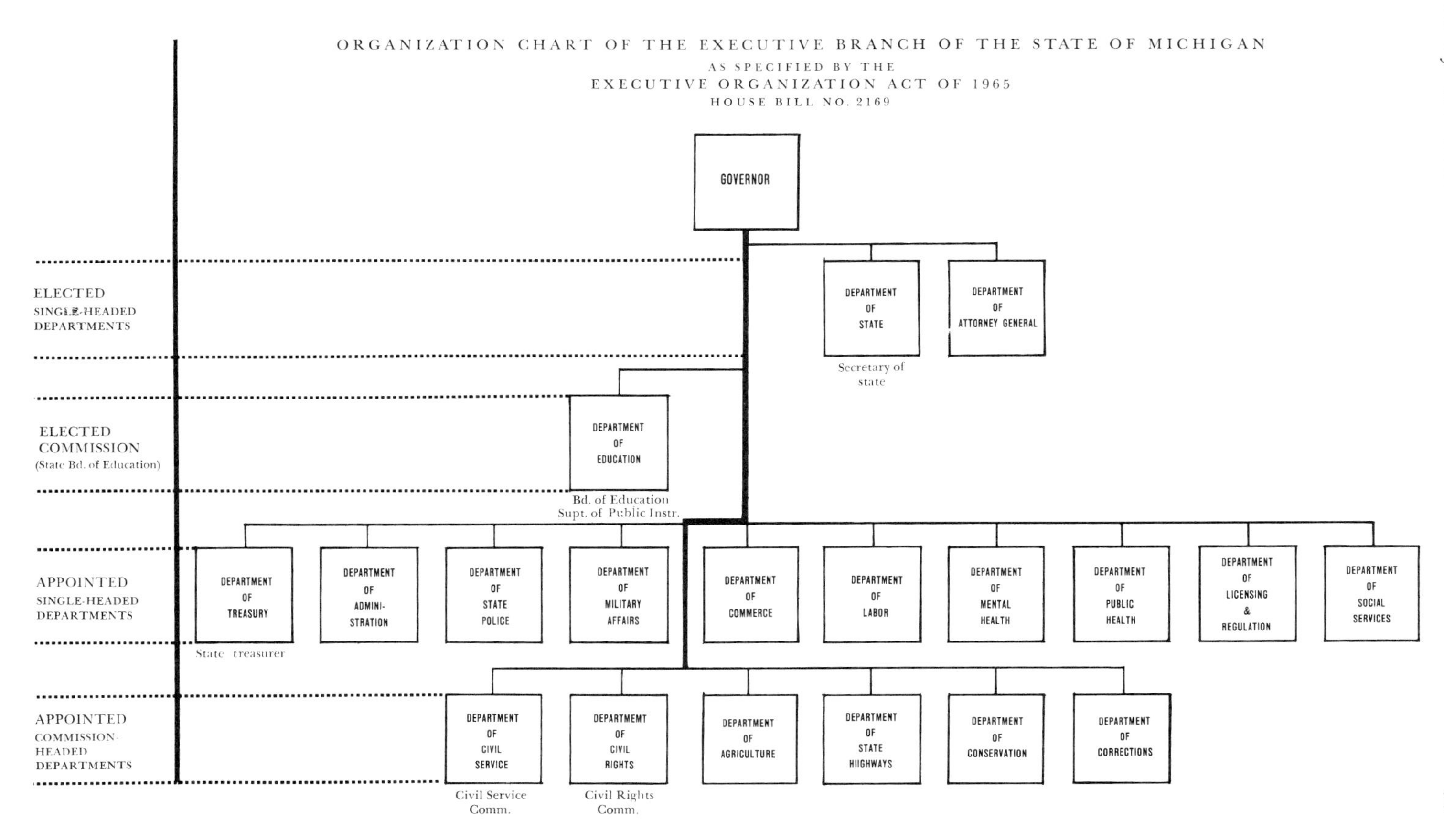
ORGANIZATION CHART OF THE EXECUTIVE BRANCH OF THE STATE OF MICHIGAN
AS SPECIFIED BY THE
EXECUTIVE ORGANIZATION ACT OF 1965
HOUSE BILL NO. 2169
GOVERNOR
ELECTED SINGLE-HEADED DEPARTMENTS
DEPARTMENT OF STATE
Secretary of state
DEPARTMENT OF ATTORNEY GENERAL
ELECTED COMMISSION (State Bd. of Education)
DEPARTMENT OF EDUCATION
Bd. of Education
Supt. of Public Instr.
APPOINTED SINGLE-HEADED DEPARTMENTS
DEPARTMENT OF TREASURY
State treasurer
DEPARTMENT OF ADMINI-STRATION
DEPARTMENT OF STATE POLICE
DEPARTMENT OF MILITARY AFFAIRS
DEPARTMENT OF COMMERCE
DEPARTMENT OF LABOR
DEPARTMENT OF MENTAL HEALTH
DEPARTMENT OF PUBLIC HEALTH
DEPARTMENT OF LICENSING & REGULATION
DEPARTMENT OF SOCIAL SERVICES
APPOINTED COMMISSION-HEADED DEPARTMENTS
DEPARTMENT OF CIVIL SERVICE
Civil Service Comm.
DEPARTMEMT OF CIVIL RIGHTS
Civil Rights Comm.
DEPARTMENT OF AGRICULTURE
DEPARTMENT OF STATE HIGHWAYS
DEPARTMENT OF CONSERVATION
DEPARTMENT OF CORRECTIONS

knowledge. It has, in Michigan and in many parts of the country, replaced the "spoils system" under which many employees of the government would lose their jobs, after election day, to persons who were friends of the winners. It was a case of "Whom do you know?" rather than "What do you know?"

Civil service workers must pass a system of examinations in order to qualify for specific jobs. An employee under civil service cannot be dismissed or promoted for political, religious, or racial reasons.

The civil service commission

The job of administering the civil service system in Michigan is the responsibility of the *civil service commission,* which consists of four members appointed by the governor. No more than two of the members can belong to the same political party. A commissioner serves for eight years, and the terms are arranged so that no more than one ends at any time.

Among the specific responsibilities of the commission are:

duties

1. placing all civil service jobs in "classifications" according to duties and responsibilities;

2. determining the salary or wage for each job classification. (The commission must notify the governor each year of increases in pay for civil service employees so that he can include them in his budget. The legislature may reduce or reject increases which have been authorized by the commission. This action requires a vote of two-thirds of the members serving in each house);

3. appointing a state personnel director on the basis of a competitive examination;

4. approving the expenditure of funds to pay state employees;

5. regulating conditions of employment for civil service workers;

6. determining the qualifications of all persons wishing civil service jobs;

7. recommending salary rates for appointed positions not in the civil service system.

The legislature is required to appropriate 1 percent of the total wages paid to civil service employees to enable the commission to do its work.

Exempt employees

Not all state employees are covered under the civil service system. Those not included are:

state employees not under civil service

1. elected officials;

2. heads of principal departments;

3. members of boards and commissions;

4. employees of courts, colleges, and universities, and the legislature;

5. members of the state armed forces;

6. eight positions in the governor's office;

7. two positions in each principal department when this is requested by the department head.

benefits

In more than two decades, over 180,000 people have been hired under civil service. Most citizens agree that the system has brought efficiency and economy to the state's administration. Civil service also seems to encourage a more secure and more professional staff of government employees.

As we have seen, the executive branch of Michigan's government is responsible for the day-to-day business of the state. It carries out the laws and regulations by which our state is governed. You should be aware of the size of this responsibility and be alert to ways the executive branch can be improved so that it might serve the people in the most far-sighted, economical, and productive manner possible.

FOR THOUGHT AND DISCUSSION

1. Michigan's governor served a two-year term for many years. The 1964 constitution, as you have read, changed this to four years. What are some of the advantages of the four-year term for the governor? Why do some citizens favor a two-year term?

2. What is the reason for the rule that salaries cannot be changed during the term of a state official?

3. Why do you think there was agreement among most of the constitutional convention delegates that the number of boards, commissions, and departments in the executive branch had to be reduced?

4. Why do some people oppose the civil service system? Why is it sometimes said that the system weakens the power of the governor?

5. Try to make a list of those state employees who are exempted from civil service. State why you think they are not included in each case.

Courtesy: Michigan Tourist Council

The cornerstone for the capitol was laid in 1873, and the building was dedicated in 1879. The total cost of construction was $1,510,310. The building contains the state senate, house of representatives, supreme court, and offices of the governor, lieutenant governor, secretary of state, attorney general, and other administrative officials.

CHAPTER VI

COURTS AND JUDGES

The Michigan Court of Justice

> Four things belong to a judge: to hear courteously, to answer wisely, to consider soberly, and to decide impartially.
>
> —Socrates

Trials, courtrooms, and judges are no longer a mystery to most people. Television has made it possible for anyone to see a fictitious trial in progress at least once a week. Recent decisions by the United States Supreme Court have made all citizens more aware of the importance of American court structure. State courts are a vital part of this structure, and in this chapter we discuss the "judicial" system of Michigan.

The Michigan "court of justice"

To understand how Michigan's courts are arranged, you should think of the judicial system as one "court of justice" with several divisions, each given certain responsibilities.

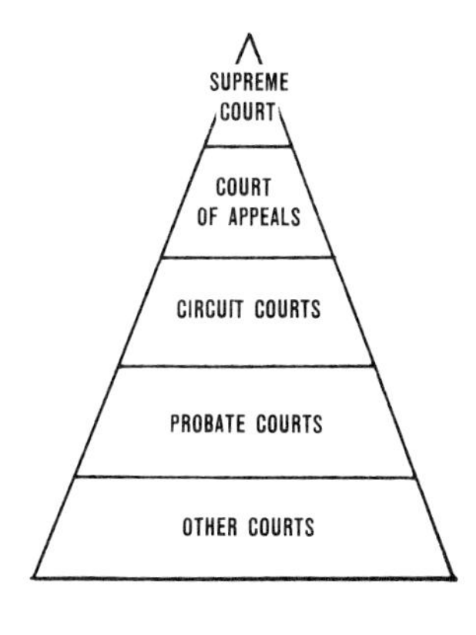

At the left is a simple diagram of the state's court of justice as established by the state constitution. There are many probate and circuit courts, one court of appeals, and one supreme court. The legislature has the power to add other divisions by a two-thirds vote of each house.

Qualifications of judges

To be a judge in any of the divisions of the Michigan court of justice, a citizen must meet several qualifications.

who can be a judge

1. He must be a lawyer, licensed to practice in the state.

2. He cannot be older than seventy. He may not be elected or appointed after reaching that age.

3. He is required to live within the area of the territory in which he was elected. If a judge moves out of this territory, he must leave office.

4. He may not be elected to any nonjudicial office during his term, or for one year after his term ends.

Judges running for reelection

Judges in Michigan are elected by the people. A judge in any of the divisions of the court of justice may run for reelection by making a sworn statement (affidavit) which states that he is a candidate for reelection. Judges who have been elected to office and are running for reelection are entitled to have the term "incumbent judge" placed under their names on the ballot. This usually helps to get votes.

Vacancies in the court

Judges may die, retire, or resign. They may also be removed from office.

impeachment of judges

Judges may be impeached for corrupt conduct and for crimes by a majority of the members serving in the house of representatives. If a judge is impeached, he is not allowed to serve in office until he is acquitted at the impeachment trial. The senate tries the impeachment and a two-thirds vote of the members serving in the senate is required for a conviction.

removal

The governor has the duty to remove judges if a resolution to do so is passed by two-thirds of the members serving in each house of the legislature. There are two requirements concerning the cause of removal.

First, the cause must be a reasonable one, and it cannot be grounds for impeachment. If such grounds do exist, the judge must be impeached.

Second, the cause must be completely stated in the resolution passed by the legislature.

filling vacancies

When a judge leaves office, a new judge is elected. A retired judge may serve in the office until the election, when appointed by the supreme court. A retired judge who fills a vacancy in this manner may not be a candidate in the election for the office.

It has been difficult to find retired judges to do this, however, and most people feel that a change is necessary.

Salaries of judges

There are four constitutional regulations concerning salaries of judges in the court of justice. They are as follows:

1. Salaries for all judges within the same division or district must be equal.

salary regulations

2. A judge's salary may not be increased or decreased during his term of office.

3. Salaries cannot be based on number of trials, fees, fines, or amount of legal activity in a judge's court. This provision was placed in the 1964 constitution because it was felt that the "fee system" was not a good one. Under this system, justices of the peace were paid according to the number of fines and other charges they were able to levy in court.

Let us now examine in some detail each of the parts of the Michigan court of justice.

THE SUPREME COURT

Powers and duties

As the highest division of Michigan's court of justice, the supreme court has great responsibility and authority. It has the power to:

1. hear appeals of cases from lower courts (All decisions by the Michigan supreme court are made by

vote and must be in writing, stating the decision and the reasons for the decision. A supreme court judge who disagrees with the decision must state his reasons in writing. Cases appealed from the supreme court of Michigan go to the United States Supreme Court in Washington, D. C.);

what does the supreme court do?

2. give advisory "opinions" on important laws after they have been passed by the legislature, but before they are scheduled to go into effect;

3. appoint a "court administrator" to carry out the various administrative duties of the court;

4. supervise the staff of the court: clerks, reporters, secretaries, etc.;

5. establish rules for practices and procedures for all divisions of the court of justice;

6. make recommendations concerning the court's financial needs each year.

Membership, election, and term

There are seven justices of the supreme court. They choose one "chief justice."

For many years, candidates for the Michigan supreme court have been nominated by political parties at their state conventions. The candidates then have run in "nonpartisan" elections; that is, they have appeared on the ballot as members of no political party. In practice, however, the political parties have usually made it clear which candidates they are supporting by mentioning them in campaign literature and advertising.

election of justices

A supreme court justice serves for eight years, and the terms of justices are arranged so that no more than two of them end at the same time.

THE COURT OF APPEALS

Membership, election, and term

First established in the 1964 constitution, the court of appeals is designed to hear appeals in many different kinds

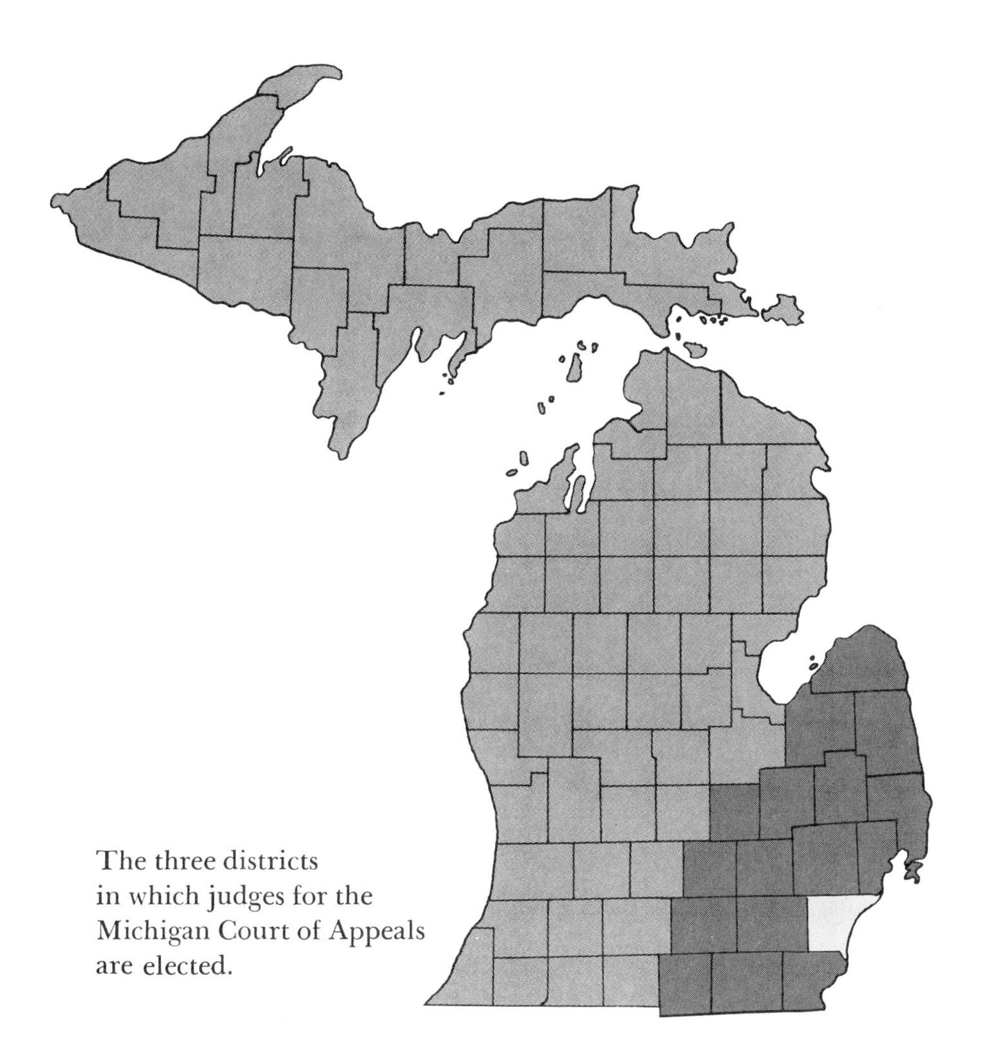

The three districts in which judges for the Michigan Court of Appeals are elected.

of cases. These appeals previously went to the supreme court, which often became overloaded.

establishing the court of appeals

The court of appeals consists of nine members, each of whom is elected from one of three districts in the state. These districts must be as equal in population as possible.

Regarding the court of appeals, the legislature has the power to:

1. increase the number of judges;

2. change the districts from which the judges are elected:

3. establish the kinds of cases over which the court will have authority.

The supreme court sets the length of court sessions and specifies where the court meets, when it meets, and whether it will be broken into divisions.

The term of a judge of the court of appeals is six years, and the terms are arranged so that not all of them end at the same time.

CIRCUIT COURTS

Powers of the circuit court

jurisdiction

The circuit courts of Michigan have broad jurisdiction. They try all cases which are not handled in any other court. Generally, cases in circuit courts involve civil suits of more than $100 and criminal cases in which the offense is a felony.

authority

They hear appeals from all lower courts, unless the legislature provides differently.

They supervise and control all lower courts according to the rules of the supreme court.

They fill vacancies in the offices of county clerk and prosecuting attorney, when these are elected offices.

It is interesting that the supreme court may require a circuit court judge to hold court in a circuit other than his own. This may be done, for example, to help a circuit court with a large load of cases.

Membership, election, and term

circuits

The state is divided, following county lines, into judicial districts called circuits. In 1967 there were forty-one circuits. The state legislature may change the number of circuits and the number of circuit judges. It *must* make changes when the supreme court feels they are necessary.

election

Circuit judges are elected in nonpartisan elections held in each district. They serve six-year terms. In circuits having more than one circuit judge, the terms are arranged so that all of them do not end at the same time.

PROBATE COURTS

Powers of the probate court

jurisdiction

The probate courts deal with cases involving the distribution of property of persons who have died, as well as the settling of their debts. The probate court decides whether a will is genuine, who is responsible for settling the estate, and who the legal heirs are.

Cases involving persons who are not mentally competent and who are placed in state institutions are usually heard in probate court.

Probate courts also handle cases involving juvenile delinquents, dependents, and the like. The legislature has the power to remove these cases from the probate court, and there has been considerable discussion in recent years about the need for a "family court" to specialize in such matters.

Membership, election, and term

Every county in Michigan has at least one probate court. The number of probate judges in a county depends principally on the population. The legislature has two powers by which it can modify the probate court districts. The legislators can:

1. create probate districts containing more than one county if this is approved by a vote of the people in each county affected;

probate districts

2. combine the office of probate judge with that of another office in the Michigan court of justice.

Both of these powers are given to the legislature to make possible more efficient court operation in smaller counties.

Probate judges are nominated and elected in non-partisan elections held within their counties or probate districts. A probate judge's term is six years. In districts where there is more than one probate judge, their terms are arranged so that all of them do not end at the same time.

election

Other courts

The constitution of 1964 gives the legislature the power to:

revising powers of the legislature

1. abolish justice of the peace courts;
2. abolish circuit court commissioners;
3. establish courts at lower levels;
4. change or abolish courts such as the recorder's court and common pleas court in Detroit, superior court in Grand Rapids, and various municipal courts in the state;
5. change or abolish the court of claims, which settles claims and demands against the state.

It will be interesting to see how the legislature establishes means by which the Michigan court of justice can handle the various kinds of cases which are brought to the courts of Michigan. Citizens should be mindful that a fair, impartial, and efficient system of justice is one of the keystones of a free society.

FOR DISCUSSION AND STUDY

1. Why do you think the "fee system" was changed in the 1964 constitution?

2. Do you think judges should be elected by the people or appointed? This makes a good debate.

3. If you were given the job of setting up the court of appeals for Michigan, how would you do it? How would you draw the districts? Would you have the court sit in different places in the state? Why?

4. Can you explain reasons for these provisions in the Michigan constitution?

   a) Retired judges who fill vacancies can't run in the election to fill the vacancy.

   b) Judges may not be elected if they are more than seventy years of age.

   c) Decisions of the supreme court must be in writing.

   d) Judges must be licensed attorneys.

5. What are some of the arguments for establishing a "family court" to deal with matters involving juveniles, dependents, and the like?

CHAPTER VII

MONEY—RAISING IT AND USING IT

Taxation and Finance

Taxes are what we pay for civilized society.

—Oliver Wendell Holmes, Jr.

Who pays for state government? Where does the state get its money? For what is the money used?

The first thing to understand about the financial affairs of the state of Michigan is that running our state is a big business. In a recent year, the state received in revenue almost one and a quarter *billion* dollars. This amount has been increasing over the years, and it seems likely that it will continue to do so.

big business

Now let's "test" ourselves on state finances for a moment. Take a piece of folded paper and, beginning with the heading "State Revenues," slide the paper down the page, line by line. As you read, try to decide what best fits in each blank space. At the end of each paragraph the correct answer appears at the right side of the page.

STATE REVENUES

The chief way of raising money for the operation of Michigan's government is by levying .... on sales, businesses, property, and specific goods.

taxes

some major revenue sources

Of all the taxes in Michigan, the .... tax brings in the most money.

sales

The tax bringing in the next greatest amount of money is the ". . . . . and weight" tax, which is used for highway purposes.

gas

Here is a source of money which you might overlook. Michigan receives money from the . . . . for such purposes as social welfare, education, highways, and hospital construction.

federal government

Other sources of revenue include a state tax on . . . ., of which two cents goes to schools, a tax on stocks, bonds, and savings accounts called the ". . . . ." tax; and earnings which the state receives on its . . . .

cigarettes
intangibles
investments

How did you do?

How is this money spent? What services does it provide for Michigan's citizens?

Test yourself again using the same method as you did with revenues.

STATE EXPENDITURES

The chief expense of Michigan's government is . . . ., including universities and colleges as well as public elementary and secondary schools.

education

a few major services

The state spends the next greatest amount on . . . . Money collected from gas and weight taxes is used for this purpose.

highways

. . . ., including aid to dependent children, aid to the blind, relief, old age benefits, and the like, is the next greatest expense.

welfare

The cost of running . . . . at the state, county, and local level is the fourth highest expenditure.

government

Care and feeding of patients, cost of running hospitals, and other expenses are grouped under . . . ., another important item in the state budget.

health

Among the other expenses which pay for services for Michigan's citizens are . . . . of natural resources, payments of money to holders of . . . ., and help to . . . . of various wars.

conservation
bonds
veterans

We have briefly examined the sources of money for the state and the services which this money provides.

Let us now look at the basic tax structure of Michigan as it is established by the state constitution. We briefly discuss the power of taxation and examine in some detail a few of the major taxes in Michigan.

The power of taxation

legislature

The Michigan legislature must pass laws imposing taxes which, when combined with other sources of revenue, will pay the expenses of our state government. The constitution requires the legislature to list each estimated amount of revenue and to keep the money-raising bills within the total of these estimates.

No money can be paid out of the state treasury except by law. Any law which levies a tax must state exactly what the tax is.

governor

The governor is required to present to the legislature a budget of proposed spending for the coming year, and he must also present ideas for raising money to meet the proposed expenses.

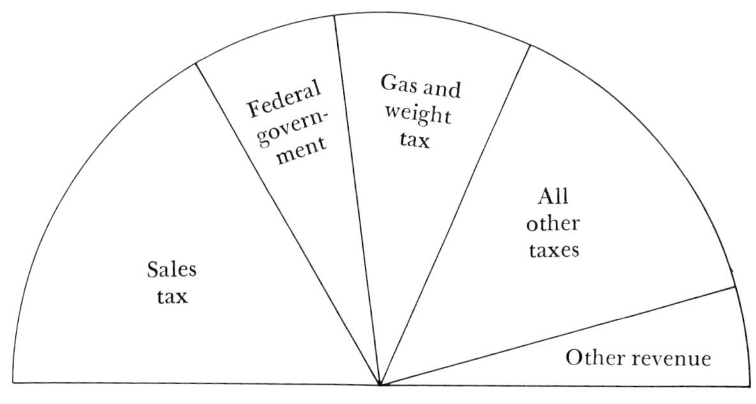

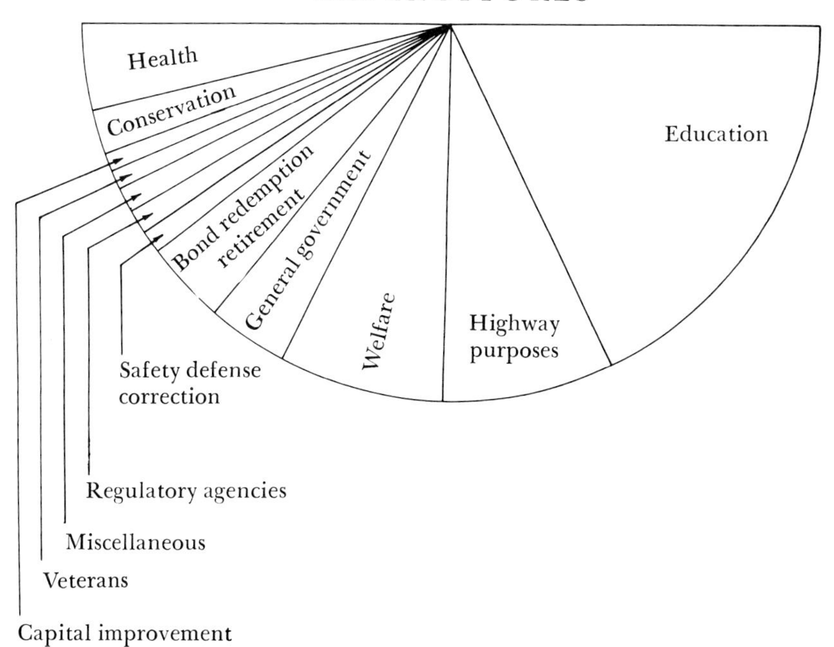

Figure IV
A typical budget of the state.

The sales tax

Almost every time you buy something in Michigan, you must "pay" a sales tax. Actually, the sales tax is paid by the seller, but he passes it on to you and his other customers. The Michigan tax is currently 4 percent, and the constitution does not permit a higher rate.

distribution of the sales tax

The money which the state collects from the sales tax is divided in the following way: one-half is spent for schools; one-eighth for cities, villages, and townships; and three-eighths for the general fund, from which the various costs of state government are paid. With a sales tax of eight cents on a $2.00 purchase, the schools get four cents, one cent is "returned" to local governments, and three cents goes to the state general fund.

The gas and weight tax

All money collected from taxes on fuels used by motor vehicles and money paid for vehicle licenses is used for highway purposes. The state legislature decides what is meant by a "highway purpose." Included are the more than 9,000 miles of state highways and over 100,000 miles of city and county roads which the state helps to maintain.

Property taxes

A chief source of income for cities, counties, townships, and villages in Michigan is the tax on real property—land, buildings, and other "improvements" on it. The Michigan constitution establishes some definite rules about property taxes in the state. Let us list some of them:

1. There can be no property tax on real estate owned and occupied by churches or schools, when the property is used only for religious or educational purposes.

rules concerning the property tax

2. Taxes on property are paid according to the value of the property. In order to determine its value, property is "assessed," or evaluated, from time to time, and a value is placed on it. This value must not be greater than 50 percent of the amount for which the property could be sold.

3. In addition to assessing the property, the county, city, village, or township must decide on the "rate" to set for property taxes. In Michigan the combined rate for counties, townships, and school districts cannot exceed fifteen dollars per $1,000 of assessed value. Thus, a person with property assessed at $10,000 would not pay more than $150 in taxes.

limit

This restriction was first placed in the Michigan constitution in the depression days of 1932 when many people were out of work and could not afford high taxes. There are a number of exceptions to this rule. Among them are:

exceptions to the limit

a) The property owners in any district may vote to increase the tax-rate limitation. This increase may place the rate as high as $50 per $1,000 of value, for a period of not more than twenty years.

b) The limitation of fifteen dollars per $1,000 of value does not apply to cities or villages.

c) If a county sets up its own form of government, the rate for property taxes is limited by the charter of the county.

Income tax

As you know, the federal government receives a large amount of money from the tax it levies on personal income—wages, salaries, etc. Michigan has not had such a tax.

Michigan income tax?

For many years, there has been a lively debate over whether the state should adopt some sort of income tax. Many people have said that it should. Some of the reasons given have been:

1. The present tax system is unfair to people who *spend* a large portion of their incomes and therefore must pay a large sales tax. Many people who say this tend to favor excluding food and drugs from the sales tax.

Yes!

2. Michigan's revenues do not meet the state's real needs. A personal income tax would add greatly to revenues.

3. Businesses are taxed too heavily in Michigan. The added income from the personal income tax would allow the state to reduce taxes on business. This would encourage business growth in Michigan.

4. An income tax would help to allow the local governments to reduce the property tax, which is now too high.

Among the arguments against a state personal income tax have been:

No!

1. The way to improve Michigan's financial situation is to reduce the money spent by the state government, not to pass a new tax.

2. A personal income tax is unfair to people with higher incomes, since they already pay a high income tax to the federal government.

3. The people of Michigan do not want it. Some of those who argue this way point to the vote on the 1960 amendment to the Michigan constitution. This amendment, which was approved by the voters by a narrow margin, raised the limit on the sales tax from 3 percent to 4 percent. It is claimed that this vote shows that the people of Michigan prefer the sales tax.

There is also an argument about what sort of personal income tax there ought to be. Should it be a "graduated" or a "flat-rate" tax?

A graduated income tax is one whose *rate* increases as the income that is taxed increases. Flat-rate means that the *percentage* each person pays is the same, regardless of income. Let us look at a brief example.

In a system of graduated income tax:

graduated tax

	Income	Rate (percent)	Income Tax
Mr. Brown	$4,000	2	$ 80.00
Mr. Green	$8,000	5	$400.00

While Mr. Green has twice as much income as Mr. Brown, he pays five times as much income tax.

In a system of flat-rate income tax:

flat-rate tax

	Income	Rate (percent)	Income Tax
Mr. Brown	$4,000	3	$120.00
Mr. Green	$8,000	3	$240.00

In this case, Mr. Green pays the same amount, in proportion to his taxable income, as does Mr. Brown.

The 1964 Michigan constitution does not permit a graduated income tax. The legislature is permitted to pass a flat-rate tax, however.

Borrowing by the state

short-term borrowing

Sometimes it is necessary for the state to borrow money. It may be that the state needs to meet a temporary shortage of funds so that it may "pay the bills." Taking on a debt for a period of one year or less is called "short-term borrowing."

The constitution of Michigan permits short-term borrowing with the following regulations.

limit

1. The amount borrowed cannot be greater than an amount equal to 15 percent of the preceding year's revenues which were not dedicated to schools, highways, local governments, etc. Currently, this restriction means that the state can borrow, for short-term purposes approximately $90,000,000.

2. The legislature must approve any such borrowing.

3. Revenues received during the year must be used to pay back the amount borrowed.

long-term borrowing rules

Long-term borrowing usually means going into debt for a specific purpose for a period of several years. The state constitution provides that long-term borrowing must: (1) be for a specific, stated purpose; (2) be approved by a two-thirds vote of the members serving in each house of the legislature; (3) be approved by a vote of the people at a general election.

Long-term borrowing in the past has been used to

acquire money for paying bonuses to veterans, for building mental hospitals, and for lending money to school districts.

A state of Michigan's size, with its many services, is a big business which requires a great deal of money. Michigan's citizens need continually to ask themselves:

> Is the burden of taxation equally spread over the state's people or are some residents paying an unfair share?
>
> Is the money well spent? Should the state change the way it is spending money for state services, either in total amount or in the manner in which the spending is done?

Informed answers to these questions can help to assure the wise use of the state's money and a profitable return on the taxpayer's dollar.

FOR DISCUSSION AND STUDY

1. Why do some people oppose the distribution of revenues from the sales tax for specific uses? Why do many people favor it?

2. Should only those people who buy licenses and gasoline pay for Michigan's highways? Develop arguments on both sides of this question.

3. Describe your views on a personal income tax for Michigan.

4. "The governor has important legislative responsibilities in the field of taxation." Explain this statement.

5. It has been said that one of Michigan's troubles is that the state's financial health is too dependent on the automobile industry. Explain.

6. An interesting report would be a description of the history of the property tax in the United States and in Michigan.

CHAPTER VIII

LOCAL GOVERNMENT

Counties

> The government is ours whether it be local, county, state or federal. It doesn't belong to anyone but the people of America. Don't treat it as an impersonal thing; don't treat it as something to sneer at; treat it as something that belongs to you.
>
> —Harry L. Hopkins

Every one of us in Michigan lives in one of its eighty-three counties. For some people the county is the closest unit of government which serves them to any great extent. Others, especially city dwellers, know only their county's name and are scarcely aware of its services.

Most Michigan county lines were drawn over a century ago. With the exception of the counties which border the Great Lakes, their shape tends to be square, especially in the Lower Peninsula. The county seat, where the court house and county offices are located, was usually placed so that a citizen could make the trip in one day on horseback.

Let us now look at the government and functions of the county in Michigan, beginning with its chief governing body.

The board of supervisors

functions

The "county board of supervisors" passes laws, establishes policy, raises money, determines the salary of county officers, and directs the general operation of county government.

represen-tation

Every township in the county is entitled to one representative on the board. The state legislature has the power to decide how cities and villages will be represented. The representation has usually been by population; the greater the population of a city, the larger its membership on the county board of supervisors.

criticisms

Some people are quite critical of the county board of supervisors system. In several counties the board has been somewhat ineffective in supervising the operation of the county. It usually meets only once or twice a month, and its members often do not have sufficient knowledge of the matters about which they make decisions. In counties with large populations, the board of supervisors can become quite large and unwieldy; Wayne County's board has had over one hundred supervisors serving on it.

However, recent court decisions have allowed counties to begin to change their boards to make them more efficient.

Elected county officials

The state constitution requires that the voters in every county elect the following officers for terms of four years:

1. A sheriff, who is the principal law enforcement officer in the county. He is usually responsible for the county jail, for the serving of legal papers, and for keeping order in the circuit court.

elected county officials

2. A prosecuting attorney, who is the county's lawyer and who represents the county in court. He brings suspected law violators to trial.

3. A county treasurer, who collects taxes, keeps tax records, and spends money according to the orders of the board of supervisors.

4. A county clerk, who keeps birth, marriage, and death statistics and records; supervises elections; issues marriage and hunting licenses; and serves as clerk of the circuit court.

5. A register of deeds, who is responsible for official records of property transactions in the county. This office is sometimes combined with the county clerk.

With the exception of the prosecuting attorney, each county official is required to have his principal office at the county seat.

Changing counties geographically

Counties may not be reduced to fewer than sixteen townships unless this is approved by the voters. Voters must approve a combination of two or more counties into a single county. Moving the county seat requires a two-thirds vote of the county board of supervisors and a majority vote of the people.

Powers and duties of county government

Counties in Michigan may:

1. Borrow money in an amount up to 10 percent of the value of property in the county;

2. Build and maintain highways and airports;

3. Regulate the construction of bridges and dams on navigable streams in the county;

4. Reorganize and combine townships under regulations set by the state legislature;

5. Do anything that can be "fairly implied" from the state constitution. This means that any reasonable power is given to a county unless it is prohibited by the state constitution or by law.

County "home rule"

Some counties in Michigan have large cities with great populations—Wayne County more than 2,500,000 people; Oakland with 690,000, are examples—while other counties have quite small populations—Keweenaw, 2,400; Oscoda, 3,400; Lake, 5,300, are examples.

The delegates who wrote the 1964 constitution agreed that it was not a good idea to require *all* counties to have the same form of government. They decided to allow any county to set up its own government under control of the legislature. The legislature has the authority to pass a law stating certain conditions that must be met by a new county government.

Let us follow the steps by which a new government for a county may be established.

steps toward county home rule

First, the legislature must pass a general law which describes the powers and limitations of any new forms of county government. The law must include: (a) a limit on the amount of property tax in the counties, (b) a restriction on the power of the counties to borrow money, and (c) a provision for the election of a charter commission to plan a new government for each county.

vote on charter

If the citizens of a county want a new form of county government, the first step is the election of a commission to write a new charter, or constitution, for the county. The voters must approve the establishment of a charter commission.

The commission writes a charter establishing the new government for the county, following the limitations made by the general law. If a majority of the voters approves the charter, the county has a new, "home-rule" government.

Townships

All Michigan counties are divided into townships. A typical county contains sixteen townships, although the number varies widely from four in Luce County to twenty-seven in Huron County.

Most organized township governments serve persons in rural areas, although in recent years new subdivisions have been built in townships on land which was formerly used for farms.

What do townships do?

basic functions

The state legislature has the authority to determine the power and duties of Michigan's townships. In the past, townships provided many services for their citizens. Today all townships supervise elections in which the residents vote, and they determine the value of property and collect taxes.

services

Many Michigan townships do no more than this. Others, usually those with larger populations, may provide water, sewage, fire protection, and building inspection. Heavily populated townships enjoy a limited "home rule" and are able to write new charters giving them greater powers to levy taxes, pass ordinances, and control certain other township affairs.

home rule

If a township falls completely within a village, the legislature dissolves the township. This is done to prevent having two local governments exactly in the same area.

Township officers

Citizens in every organized township elect a "township board," which acts as the legislative and executive branches of government. The board is made up of the following officials:

elected township officers

1. A supervisor, who represents the township on the county board of supervisors, and who also is responsible for assessing property;
2. A clerk, who keeps records, registers voters, and often supervises elections;
3. A treasurer, who collects taxes and keeps the financial records of the township;
4. No more than four trustees, who serve on the township board and participate in its decisions.

Cities and Villages

Situated on the Rifle River in Arenac County, Omer, the smallest city in Michigan, had a population of 322 in the last census. In the same year (1960), the largest city in the state was Detroit with a population of more than 1,670,000. What do you think is the population of the largest village in the state? How many people live in the smallest village? The village of Inkster in Wayne County had more than

39,000 residents in 1960, and Grand Beach, a city at the far southwestern corner of the state, had a population of eighty-six.

Cities and villages in Michigan have had *home rule* for more than fifty-five years. Our state was the seventh in the nation to allow these governments to be established according to local needs under some control by the state legislature. The general home rule law limits the property tax rate and the amount of debt a city or village may have.

municipal home rule

Since 1909 almost half of the cities and villages in Michigan have adopted charters, and it is generally agreed that our state has had great success with home rule. The process for writing home-rule charters for cities and villages follows a procedure similar to that for counties—a charter commission is approved and elected. It then writes a charter which must be approved by the voters.

Special powers of cities and villages

The state constitution gives specific powers to cities and villages in addition to the power to write their own charters. Among the specific powers are:

1. the right to own public works which promote health and safety, such as hospitals, parks, and water purification plants;

what cities may do

2. the authority to own and operate service facilities for supplying water, light, power, sewage disposal, and transportation;

3. the right to provide service facilities to people who live outside the city or village limits;

4. the power to pass necessary laws which do not conflict with the constitution or state laws.

Forms of city government

Under home rule the citizens in more than 180 cities have voted to establish the form of government which seems best suited to the needs of the community.

These forms of organization fall into four basic cate-

gories. The most common is the *council-manager plan,* which is used in over one hundred cities in the state. In this type of city government the voters elect a city council, which appoints a city manager, who is a professional administrator responsible for the day-to-day operations of the city. The city council passes laws for the city.

council-manager

Quite popular in the larger cities of the state has been the *strong-mayor plan,* in which the mayor and city council are elected. The mayor appoints most of the city officials, and is responsible for the daily operation of the city government.

strong mayor

The *weak-mayor plan* is the oldest form of city government. Here the mayor has comparatively little power and the city council has a great deal. Usually, the mayor can appoint and remove officials only with the consent of the council, and the mayor generally has little control over the many functions of city government. There are still a few Michigan cities which have this kind of government.

weak mayor

The *commission form* has recently become less popular in Michigan. In this type of city government, elected commissioners act together to pass laws for the city. In addition, these commissioners serve as heads of individual city departments—water, health, public safety, and the like.

commission

Metropolitan areas

Cities usually are surrounded by suburbs consisting of villages, well-populated townships, and other cities. These areas often grow to be large and are called "metropolitan areas." A metropolitan area is defined by the United States Census Bureau as a county or group of counties forming a center of population and containing a city of 50,000 people. According to the most recent census, Michigan's ten metropolitan areas include the following cities: Detroit, Flint, Grand Rapids, Lansing, Saginaw, Jackson, Ann Arbor, Kalamazoo, Muskegon-Muskegon Heights, and Bay City.

Michigan's metropolitan areas

Metropolitan areas often have problems of water supply, sewage disposal, transportation, planning, and air pollution and other problems which are also common to all residents of the area. For example, a river flowing through several communities might be a source of water for all of them. They might decide that they need a new unit of government to manage the water supply most efficiently.

new forms of government

The Michigan constitution allows the legislature to establish forms of government with powers to deal with such problems and functions. In order to prevent too many government units from being formed, each one must deal with as many functions as possible.

use of existing governments

The constitution also provides that metropolitan areas may attempt to solve their problems by *cooperation* among existing counties, cities, townships, and villages. These governmental bodies may agree to provide services for each other, share expenses, transfer duties, and cooperate in other ways to meet common needs.

FOR DISCUSSION AND STUDY

1. Do you live in a city, a village, or a township? Where does your governing body meet? How often? Plan a visit to observe one of its meetings. It would be a good idea to plan for the visit before you go; find out who the members are, what their occupations and major interests are, etc. You should try to learn about the kinds of things which will be discussed at the meeting. These steps will help to make the meeting meaningful.

2. Why is a limit on county property tax usually felt to be desirable?

3. Examine again the brief descriptions of the forms of city government. List several advantages and disadvantages of each form. Try to decide why some types of government are becoming more popular than others.

4. Describe some examples which illustrate the need for special metropolitan governments.

CHAPTER IX

THE PEOPLE ACT

Direct Democracy in Michigan

> The government is ours; we are the government, you and I.
>
> —Theodore Roosevelt

In a democracy, the first responsibility for the government lies with the people. If they are alert, interested, and active in public affairs, the government will represent them successfully. If there are many citizens who "don't have time," "don't understand," or "don't care," the elected officials in Washington, in Lansing, and in local areas will find it difficult to reflect their points of view. Government leaders will be more likely to listen to the few who take the time to make themselves heard.

There are, of course, many ways by which the people can influence the government. We have already discussed voting and its importance. Another effective way is by taking an active interest in political life. This is such an interesting and important matter that we devote a separate chapter to it.

influencing the government

Many people influence the government by writing letters, making telephone calls, and sending telegrams to their representatives. They often try to get other people to do so. All persons have the right to circulate petitions asking their government officials to do (or not to do) something.

In this chapter, we discuss briefly three other ways by which the people can act directly on government. These are the *initiative, referendum,* and *recall.* We will see how citizens can amend the constitution. Each of these powers gives the citizens of Michigan, acting by themselves, the opportunity to change the government without having to depend on the elected officials for such changes.

INITIATIVE

What is the initiative?

The initiative is the power of the people to make and reject laws.

How can the people make laws?

Suppose you (a citizen at least eighteen years old) wish to propose a law to lower the driving age in Michigan. What are the steps to be followed?

1. You must circulate petitions stating the exact wording of the law you are proposing. Only registered voters are allowed to sign a petition.

2. You then take your petitions to the proper state official in Lansing—usually the secretary of state. If there are enough proper signatures, he approves the petitions. The number of signatures must equal 8 percent of the total vote for governor in the last election.

3. You then present your signed petitions to the state legislature. The next step is up to the state senators and representatives. They may: (a) enact your proposal into law, (b) reject your proposal, or (c) make a different proposal for a law about the driving age.

If your proposal is not enacted into law within forty days of the time you present it to the legislature, it must be voted on by the people at the next general election.

If the legislature makes a different proposal, both it and your proposal are placed on the ballot and the one receiving the most "yes" votes becomes the law.

Laws adopted by the initiative cannot be vetoed by the governor. They cannot be amended or repealed unless:

1. The law itself expressly provides for amendment or repeal;

2. The voters approve amendment or repeal, or

3. Three-fourths of the members serving in each house of the legislature vote for amendment or repeal.

Although the initiative has not often been used to propose laws in Michigan, it is an important power for the people to have. It helps to remind the state legislators that the people may act when they feel that the lawmakers have not.

REFERENDUM

What is the referendum?

The referendum is the power of the people to approve or reject laws which have been passed by the legislature. During the ninety-day period after the adjournment of the legislature, the people, by petition, may require that a law passed during the session be voted on at the next general election.

How do the people exercise the right of referendum?

referendum process

The petitioning process for the referendum is similar to that for the initiative, except that the number of signatures required is only 5 percent of the total vote for governor at the last election.

When the petitions have enough signatures and have been submitted to the proper official, the law is voted on at the next general election. The law cannot go into effect until it is approved by the voters. If it is not approved, it cannot become a law. Laws passed to raise money for state institutions or to make up deficits in state funds do not come under the power of referendum.

use of referendum

Since 1930 the people and the legislature of Michigan have used the referendum on ten occasions. Seven times the voters have rejected the law and three times the law has been adopted. A referendum vote has been held on laws dealing with such subjects as the manufacture and sale of oleomargarine, a tax on cigarettes, and the requiring of foreign agents to register in the state.

RECALL

What is recall?

Recall is the power of the people to remove from office any elected official, except a judge, for any reason.

How does recall operate in Michigan?

how recall works

An official is removed from office by a vote of the people at a special recall election. The voters are asked whether the official should be "recalled." If a majority votes "yes," the official is removed from office, and a special election is then held to fill the vacancy.

Recall elections must be held when citizens sign petitions asking for the removal of an official. The number of signatures required must equal 25 percent of the most recent vote for governor in the official's district. This is a large number of signatures, and the recall is not used very often in Michigan. But the fact that the people have the right to remove poor officials from office is important.

AMENDING THE CONSTITUTION

We have already seen that the legislature has the power to propose amendments to the state constitution. These proposals must be approved by a vote of the people.

The people of the state also have the right to propose amendments. This is done by petition.

Suppose that you are a registered voter and that you wish to start the procedure for amending the constitution to allow for a lower voting age in Michigan. What are the steps involved in this process?

1. You must circulate petitions stating the exact wording of the amendment you propose.

steps in amending the state constitution

2. Your petitions can be signed by registered voters only. The total number of signatures must equal at least 10 percent of the votes cast for all candidates for governor in the most recent election.

3. The petitions must be completed and turned in to the proper state official at least 120 days before the

general state election in which you want the citizens to vote on your proposal.

4. If the petitions have enough proper signatures, the proposed amendment is placed on the ballot. The purpose of the proposal must be stated in not more than one hundred words.

5. If more votes are cast in favor of the proposal than against it, it becomes an amendement to the state constitution, effective forty-five days after the election. If two amendments dealing with the same subject are passed in the same election, the one receiving the most "yes" votes is the one which will become effective.

Between 1909 and 1962, the Michigan constitution was amended fifty-nine times by proposals originated by the legislature and ten times by petition. Fifty-seven proposals, mostly from the legislature, were rejected by the people. In recent years the constitution has been amended to raise the limitation of the sales tax, to change the name of Michigan State University, and to allow the state to pay bonuses to veterans of the Korean War. A recent vote on a constitutional amendment was in November 1966, when the citizens voted against lowering the voting age to eighteen.

examples

The constitution requires that the voters of the state have the right to vote regularly on the question, "Should a convention be called to revise the state constitution?" This question will be automatically placed on the ballot every sixteen years beginning in 1978. If there are more "yes" than "no" votes, a convention will be held. Delegates will be chosen in partisan elections, and the people must vote on the revised document.

FOR DISCUSSION AND STUDY

1. What reasons can you give to explain the differences in the number of signatures required on petitions for initia-

tive, for referendum, and for recall? Why does recall require many more signatures?

2. Why do you think the delegates decided to require that the question of whether to hold a constitutional convention must be placed on the ballot every sixteen years?

3. The initiative, referendum, and recall are sometimes called the "weapons of the people." Explain this statement.

4. Should elections to select delegates to a constitutional convention be partisan or nonpartisan? There are good arguments on each side and it makes an interesting debate.

Courtesy: University of Michigan Photographic Service

An aerial view of The University of Michigan in Ann Arbor.

CHAPTER X

"THE MEANS OF EDUCATION . . ."

Schools in Michigan

> The direction in which education starts a man will determine his future life.
>
> —Plato
> *The Republic*

"Religion, morality, and knowledge being necessary to good government and the happiness of mankind, schools and the means of education shall forever be encouraged."

These words have long appeared in the Michigan constitution. Read them again. They describe the importance the people of our state place in education. Originally, these words were in the Northwest Ordinance, the law by which the territory of Michigan and of her neighbors was established by the federal government in the early days of our nation.

importance of education

In the century and a half since the beginning of schools in Michigan, overwhelming interest of the state's citizens has resulted in the creation of an enormous system of public schools, the establishment of a large number of private institutions, and the development of a set of colleges and universities of which Michigan can be justly proud.

One more section from Michigan's constitution should be quoted directly. It reads:

> The legislature shall maintain and support a system of free public elementary and secondary schools as defined by law. Every school district shall provide for the education of its pupils without discrimination as to religion, creed, race, color or national origin.

This section requires Michigan to have a system of free public schools. It also forbids any school district to discriminate on the basis of religion, creed, race, color, or national origin. The writers of the 1964 constitution worked at a time when racial discrimination in schools, particularly in the South, was a topic of vital public interest. This section leaves no doubt where the state of Michigan stands on this question.

We now know (1) that Michigan's people have long held education to be of great importance, (2) that public and private education in our state has thrived in the fertile soil of this great public interest, and (3) that the people of Michigan are agreed that discrimination has no place in public education.

Now let us see how Michigan's schools are organized and supervised.

Local boards of education

local responsibility

In Michigan the people run their own public schools. There are approximately 1200 school districts covering the state, and in each district the voters elect a board of education. Each local board of education has the responsibility of setting policies, raising money, and serving as general supervisor for the schools in that district.

At the state level the Michigan system of education is organized by the constitution and placed into operation by the legislature.

The state board of education

authority

The responsibility of *planning* and *coordinating* all public education from kindergarten through college is placed in the state board of education. The board also has *supervision* over all public education except those colleges or universities which have the legal power to grant bachelor's degrees. Degree-granting institutions have their own "boards of control" which supervise their operations. The state board of education is required to advise the legislature concerning the amounts of money required each year by the system of public education.

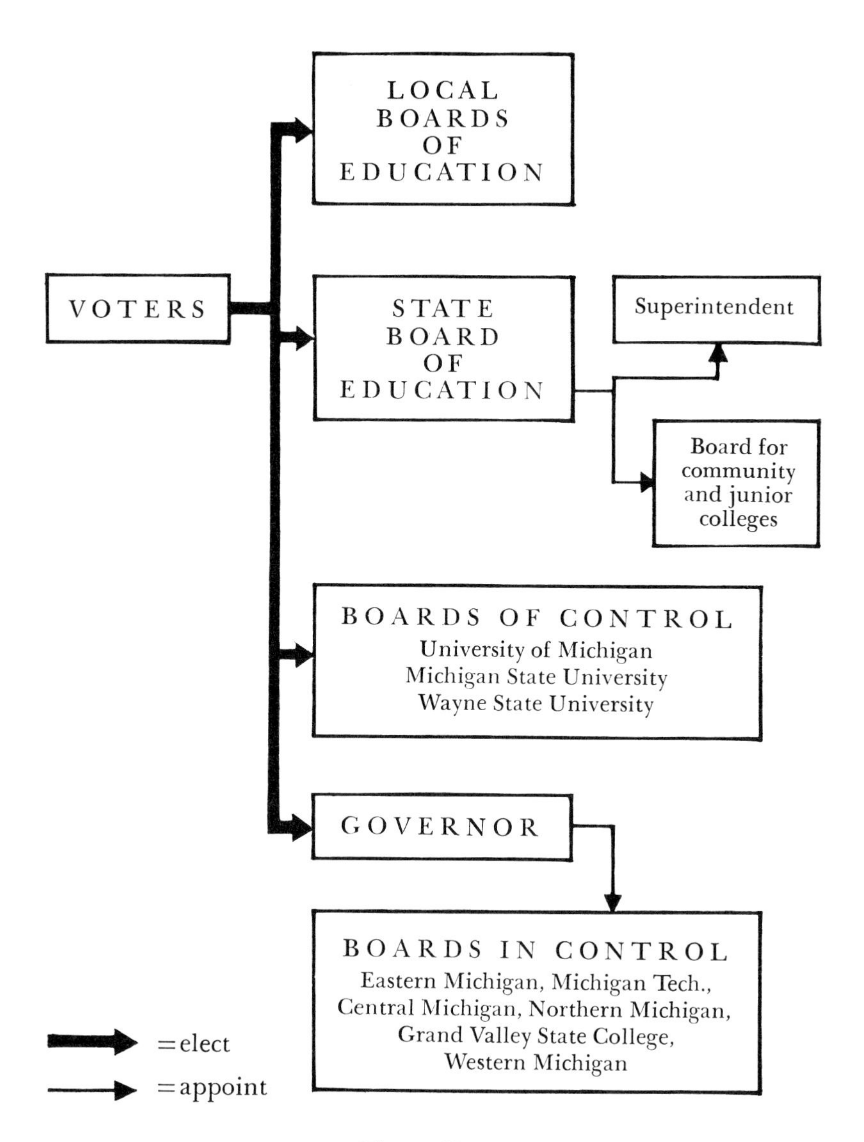

Figure V
Education in Michigan.

There are eight members of the state board of education. The term of a member of the board is eight years and the terms are arranged so that no more than two end at the same time.

member-ship

Candidates for the board are nominated at political party conventions every two years and are elected by a vote of the people of the state in each November general election. In addition to the eight members elected by the people, there are two other members of the board who have no vote but may participate in discussions of the board. They are the governor, who is a member by virtue of his office, and the superintendent of public instruction, whom we shall discuss next.

The superintendent of public instruction

While the state board of education establishes policies for education in the state, the superintendent of public instruction is responsible for carrying them out. He is the chief educational official of the state. Let us list some of his responsibilities:

duties of the superin-tendent

1. He is in charge of the state department of education, which has a staff to administer the state school law and to advise local school systems.

2. He advises the governor on educational matters.

3. He serves as chairman of the state board of education.

4. He carries out the policies of the state board of education and the laws passed by the legislature which concern schools.

The superintendent of public instruction is chosen by the state board of education. The board decides the length of his term of office.

Colleges and universities

It was pointed out earlier that colleges and universities with legal authority to grant bachelor's degrees have their own boards of control. These boards have various responsibilities, among which are:

1. general supervision of the college or university;

boards for institutions of higher education

2. control of money spent by the school. This money comes from various sources; funds raised by the legislature, gifts from business enterprises, grants by the federal government, contributions from individuals, and fees paid by students.

3. selection of a president for the college or university. The president is the chief executive of the school and a member of the board of control. He has no vote.

membership

A member of a board of control of a college or university serves an eight-year term. Each board has eight members and their terms are arranged so that no more than two end at the same time. Board meetings must be open to the public.

The voters of Michigan elect the boards of control for the three largest state universities. These are the regents of The University of Michigan; the board of trustees of Michigan State University; and the board of governors of Wayne State University. Members of the boards of control of the other colleges and universities are appointed by the governor with the approval of the senate.

The legislature is required to raise money to maintain the following universities and colleges in the state:

1. The University of Michigan, in Ann Arbor, composed of seventeen schools and colleges from which more than a quarter of a million persons have graduated, recognized as one of America's leading universities;

2. Michigan State University, with a beautiful campus in East Lansing, which has developed from the first agricultural college in America to one of the most important and fastest growing universities in the Midwest;

"constitutional" universities and colleges

3. Wayne State University, in Detroit, whose dramatic building program in recent years has reflected its role as an educational and cultural center in the Detroit metropolitan area;

4. Eastern Michigan University, Ypsilanti, which is primarily a school for teacher preparation;

5. Michigan College of Science and Technology, in Houghton, offering a wide range of scientific and technical training, founded in 1885;

6. Central Michigan University, in Mount Pleasant, originally a teacher's college but now a many-purpose university;

7. Northern Michigan University, in Marquette, training over 5,000 students in programs of a teaching and preprofessional nature;

8. Western Michigan University, in Kalamazoo, a rapidly growing teacher-training and technical school serving primarily the southwestern part of the state;

9. Ferris Institute, in Big Rapids, whose primary emphasis is in practical, vocational, and technical education;

10. Grand Valley State College, near Grand Rapids, a new school taking its place among Michigan's institutions of higher learning.

The legislature must also provide funds for any colleges or universities which may be established in the future under state support. The rapid rise in the number of young people entering institutions of higher learning makes likely the creation of such schools.

Community and junior colleges

In several places in Michigan local colleges have been organized to meet the needs of high-school graduates who do not go on to a state college or university, but who wish to continue their education. These "community colleges" or "junior colleges" are supervised by boards elected in the city or county which the school serves.

The legislature is required to pass laws regulating the establishment and financial support of such colleges. To help supervise, plan, and advise the system of community colleges, the state board of education appoints a "state board for public community and junior colleges." Board members serve eight years and their terms are arranged so that no more than two end at the same time. By virtue of his office, the state superintendent is a member of the board. He has no vote.

Other educational programs

In addition to the system of public schools, colleges, and universities, there are many other educational programs for which the state has a responsibility. These include driver training, adult education, instructional programs in state hospitals and prisons, programs and services for the physically and mentally handicapped, and libraries.

FOR THOUGHT AND DISCUSSION

1. What are the advantages of appointing a state superintendent of public instruction rather than having him elected by the people? Why do some citizens prefer the election of a superintendent?

2. At present a state law requires each child to attend school until the age of sixteen. Why do you think we have this law? Do you think the age should be changed? How? Explain your answer.

3. Every student in Michigan must complete at least one semester of American government in order to graduate from high school. Is this a good requirement? Would you add others?

4. "Resolved, that a college student should be required to pay one-half of the cost of his education." Debate this question. You will be surprised at the variety of opinions on the subject!

Developing, conserving, and protecting our natural resources is a year-round job.

A Michigan conservation department officer gives directions to two hunters.

A state forester takes a boring to determine a tree's age and health.

A geologist takes a rock sample for study from a quarry in southern Michigan.

A Michigan stream is "planted" with young fish.

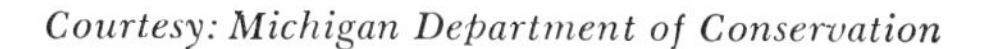

Courtesy: Michigan Department of Conservation

CHAPTER XI

PARTIES AND PEOPLE

Politics in Michigan

Politics is the art of government.

—Harry Truman

Pick up your local newspaper. The chances are that it will contain "political news." It might be that one party is blaming the other for a traffic problem, for a lack of action in smoke control, or for a policy of softness on communism. A citizen may be announcing his candidacy for a government office. A party might be making a statement about a current issue.

Sometimes it might seem that political parties are always arguing.

Did you ever think that this might be a good sign? We know that individuals disagree quite often. If the parties never disagreed about anything, it might be an indication that they were not really representing the views of their members.

In the United States we have a two-party system. In some parts of the country, however, one party is almost always in power. This has been true, for example, of the Republican party in sections of New England and in areas of the Middle West; however, some Southern states have been strongly Democratic for many years.

parties in Michigan

Today Michigan has an excellent two-party system, since the parties are well established and approximately equal in strength.

For many years Michigan was Republican, but gradually over the past four decades the Democrats have become important in Lansing. In the 1925 legislature there were

Republican and Democratic strength

131 Republicans and no Democrats; in 1931 Republicans outnumbered Democrats, 129 to 3. Two years later, the 72 Democrats were numerically superior to the 60 Republicans; in 1945 there were 90 Republicans and 42 Democrats; in 1959, 77 Republicans and 67 Democrats. In the 1961 legislature there was one more Republican and one less Democrat than in 1959. In the election of 1966 the Republicans took control of the senate, and the house was evenly divided between the two parties.

Since the Civil War, there have been twenty-two Republican and seven Democratic governors. A Democrat, G. Mennen Williams, held the office from 1949 to 1961. Combined with the increase in the size of cities, this aided the rise of the Democratic party in Michigan. The election of George Romney to the governorship in 1962, 1964, and 1966 helped to restore the confidence of Michigan's Republicans in their party's strength.

Most people agree that a healthy two-party system helps make sure that we have good government. If one party seems to be doing an unsatisfactory job in office, the voters will be able to turn to the other party for leadership. This tends to keep both organizations alert to the wishes of the citizens. Improvements in the operation of state government come about more frequently in states having strong two-party systems.

There have been times when third parties have been successful and have had a stimulating effect on the voters, the government, and the other political groups.

We sometimes think of politicians only as important people holding positions in government, yet thousands of Michigan's citizens spend many hours doing political work —most without pay. Why do they do it? There seem to be many reasons. Let us list a few.

why are people active in politics?

1. These "volunteers" feel that being active in a political party is a service to the community. They believe that good government is important and they are eager to work for it.

2. Some citizens have particular interests or points of view, and they hope to influence the government

and other citizens. By being active in politics they feel that they have a better chance to express their views effectively.

3. Many people enjoy the social part of politics. They like working with others in a common cause, and they appreciate the social events which political parties often sponsor. Political activity is a good way to meet people.

4. Some active party workers are students of government and wish to observe its operation firsthand.

5. Some individuals wish to run for public office. They become active in political work in order to become well-known among party members.

6. There are few political party workers who can resist the excitement of an important nominating convention or the suspense of an election night when the votes are being counted. It is a great satisfaction to be part of a winning campaign.

There are other reasons—a desire for government employment, prestige, a wish to associate with famous people, and family tradition. The major political parties are composed of people from all walks of life, with various sorts of backgrounds.

SERVICES OF POLITICAL PARTIES

Selecting candidates

One of the chief services that political parties perform is to nominate candidates for office. This might take place in someone's living room, when a group of citizens ask a neighbor to run for city council or township board. It might happen in a crowded hall, when the delegates to a state convention decide on a candidate for attorney general. Or it might occur in the privacy of the voting booth, when the party members, in a primary, decide who will be their candidate for governor. In each case the active party workers and other interested citizens are making a vital decision—who shall run?

nomination

Parties on the ballot

Imagine that you are organizing a political party and that your party wishes to run candidates for state offices in the next election. To be eligible to place your party and its candidates on the ballot, you must file a petition with the secretary of state at least six months before the election. This petition must:

getting a party on the ballot

1. request the placing of the party on the ballot;
2. be signed by registered voters equal to more than 1 percent and less than 4 percent of the votes received by the candidate elected secretary of state in the last general election. According to the 1960 and 1962 elections, respectively, the minimum number of signatures was 17,538 and 14,895;
3. be signed by at least one-hundred residents in each of ten counties;
4. have no more than 35 percent of the minimum required from any one county.

staying on and returning to the ballot

Once your party has been placed on the ballot, it is entitled to keep appearing as long as your "principal candidate" receives at least 1 percent of the votes cast for the person elected secretary of state in the last general election. "Principal candidate" usually means the candidate for governor; however, if your party did not run anyone for governor, "principal candidate" means the candidate first appearing in your party column on the ballot.

If your party does not receive at least the required 1 percent, it cannot automatically appear on the ballot. If you wish it to appear on the ballot again, you must go through the same procedure as when you placed your party on the ballot the first time.

In Michigan there are several minor parties which usually fail to meet the 1 percent requirement at each election. For example, in 1958 the requirement to appear on the ballot was 15,315 votes for the principal candidate in the 1956 election. The principal candidate of the Prohibition party received 6538 votes. The Prohibition party petitioned again and in 1962 it appeared on the ballot.

Other services of political parties

In addition to selecting and running candidates for the various offices in the state, political parties perform a variety of other important jobs.

other party services

1. They raise and help to make clear the issues which are under debate in the election.

2. They perform all sorts of voter services—helping people to get to the polls, babysitting on election day, etc.

3. They help to publicize elections by announcements and advertisements in behalf of candidates.

4. They give voters information about registration, voting places, etc.

How are political parties organized?

Party organization in Michigan is quite complicated. Let us examine a few important state requirements about the structure of political groups in Michigan.

The voters in each party have the responsibility of electing to a county convention delegates who represent the voting area in which they live. Party county conventions meet each year. They have the important job of selecting delegates to the state convention. Each county is entitled to a number of delegates to the state convention in proportion to the most recent vote cast for secretary of state in the county.

The county convention also passes "resolutions" expressing the views of the delegates on local, state, national, and international issues.

The *state convention* has three important jobs:

1. It nominates candidates for state office—lieutenant governor, secretary of state, attorney general, the supreme court, university boards of control, and the state board of education.

2. It selects a state central committee, which supervises the state party and conducts its affairs. The state

state convention

central committee consists of seventy-six members—two men and two women from each of Michigan's nineteen districts which are represented by United States congressmen.

national convention

3. Every four years the state convention selects delegates to the party's national convention at which candidates for President and vice-president are chosen. It also selects "electors" to cast electoral votes for President and vice-president.

County organization

the county committee

A political party in a county is organized into a county committee, which is a sizeable group having the responsibility of carrying out the various political tasks in the county. These tasks include conducting campaigns, some supervision of the local organizations, and many other matters. The selection of the members of the county committee is made by an executive committee. This group is made up of (1) the candidates for the state legislature and county offices, and (2) an equal number of other persons. The executive committee selects members of the county committee on the basis of either of two plans; two members per township and two per ward in each city, or two per precinct throughout the county.

You can see that there are many ways for a person to be chosen as an official member of a political party. But there are many other ways to help a party of your choice. The list is practically endless, but let us suggest a few.

ways to help your party

1. You might offer to help the political workers in your neighborhood. This might include checking people's party interests, determining if voters are registered, circulating petitions, collecting money, passing out literature for candidates, addressing envelopes, or representing your party as a "poll-watcher" on election day.

2. You might attend meetings of your party, at which you will have the chance to express your opinions. One of the most interesting things about politics is the

great variety of opinions within our two major political parties. The debates about the position a party should take often become quite lively, heated, and interesting. These meetings might be in your precinct, ward, city, township, or county.

3. You might serve on a special committee to study a community problem and help to decide what position your party ought to take.

4. You could run for office! You might be surprised at the problem the parties have in getting people to be candidates in some areas. Running for political office is a unique experience. A candidate has the opportunity to meet many new people, and is helping his community by performing an important public service.

With the exception of the last one, each of the above is an activity which can be engaged in by persons who are not old enough to vote. Many local political parties have young groups which work with older members, and willing workers are always welcome.

young groups

No discussion of participation in political life is complete without a mention of the important contribution of women. More and more women are running for office and are assuming responsibility for leadership in political parties. In many areas women make political organizations work. They address envelopes, make telephone calls, ring doorbells, make up and type lists of party voters, check registrations, and do most of the daily jobs which help to make political parties an important force in American life.

Taking an active part in political life is not always easy. The work can be hard and the hours long, especially before elections. Yet thousands of people contribute time and energy to politics because they feel that they are making an important contribution to democracy. They are.

FOR DISCUSSION AND STUDY

1. Why must parties receive 1 percent of the vote in order to remain on the ballot? Why do you think there are so many requirements concerning the petitioning?

2. Politics is sometimes dishonest, and people still tend to suspect "politicians." Fortunately, Michigan has not had many examples of dishonest politics. How can citizens insure that the state will remain this way?

3. You might arrange to visit a local political meeting and report to the class about your experience. Perhaps someone else could go to a meeting of another party, and you could compare notes.

4. Interview candidates. If you can, talk to two candidates for the same office. See how they differ on various issues, how they view the office they are seeking, etc. Report to the class.

5. Clip all news of politics and government from newspapers and magazines and post on the bulletin board. You may be surprised at the amount!

6. Invite an active party-worker to talk to the class. Find out more about what political work is like.

7. There are several other parties in addition to the Republicans and the Democrats. What do they believe? You might read their platforms and report on them, or invite one of their members to speak to the class.

A LOOK AHEAD

The people of Michigan have taken a fresh look at their state government, and have adopted a new state constitution. But problems remain.

Michiganders join with other Americans in concern over the threat of nuclear war, the possibilities for disarmament, the need for improved relations between the races, and many other vexing situations of the day.

In their own state, Michigan's people from Lake Erie to Lake Superior are wrestling with numerous state and local problems. Among them are the following:

1. How can the rate of unemployment be reduced, particularly in Detroit and the Upper Peninsula, and among young people and minority groups?

2. What can be done about the yearly slaughter of men, women, and children on the state's highways?

3. How can citizens best plan for the proper use of our lakes, streams, forests, and other natural resources so that the vital needs of future generations will be met?

4. By what means can the state promote the education of all of its young people so that they may be able to develop themselves and take their places as active, intelligent citizens?

5. How can we best solve problems which affect Michigan *and* other states?

6. How can the goals of "freedom and justice for all" be reached in Michigan?

Thoughtful answers to these and other questions seem necessary to assure Michigan's future as a prosperous, scenic, and progressive state.

ANNOTATED BIBLIOGRAPHY

Listed here are several books which the student and the teacher will find helpful in adding to their knowledge of Michigan and its government.

Baird, Willard. *This Is Our Michigan.* Battle Creek: Federated Publications, Inc., 1960.

Facts and figures of all kinds about resources, history, places, schools, etc., in Michigan told in capsule form.

Bald, F. Clever. *Michigan in Four Centuries.* New York: Harpers, Inc., 1961.

An excellent, well-written history of the state. This book is a "must" for citizens interested in Michigan's past.

Brown, David S. *A Governor's Residence for Michigan?* Ann Arbor: University of Michigan Institute of Public Administration, 1961.

A brief account of arguments, with facts and figures showing various aspects of the question.

Citizens Research Council of Michigan. *The Proposed Michigan Constitution.* Detroit, 1962.

A "three-strip" book—one for the new constitution, one for the 1908 document, and one for comments about the differences between the two. Each article is done, section by section, in this way. A definitive, complete work.

Citizens Research Council of Michigan. *A Comparative Analysis of the Michigan Constitution.* Volumes I and II. Detroit, 1961.

Comments, notes, and history on all the parts of the 1908 constitution. It also contains comparisons with other state documents and suggestions for change, some of which were incorporated into the 1964 constitution.

Michigan Constitutional Convention. *Journal of Proceedings.*

The daily record of work on the floor of the convention.

Constitutional Convention of Michigan. *What the Proposed New State Constitution Means to You.* Lansing, 1962.

The official "report to the people" by the delegates of the convention. The booklet contains the full text of the 1964 constitution, with explanatory notes after each section. There is also a summary of major points of change.

Inter-University Faculty Committee on Constitutional Revision. *The Proposed Michigan Constitution: Analyses and Interpretations.* Ann Arbor.

A set of opinions on eight features of the new constitution.

LaPalombara, Joseph. *Guide to Michigan Politics.* East Lansing: Bureau of Social and Political Research, Michigan State University, 1960.

A detailed account of the subject by a political scientist. It gives the reader the "ins and outs" of politics in the state.

League of Women Voters of Michigan. *Know Your State*. Detroit, 1957.
A treatment of state government under the 1908 constitution.

League of Women Voters of Michigan. *It's Your Choice*. Detroit, 1962.
A discussion of the vote on the new constitution which points out, in the main, the strong points of the 1964 document from the point of view of the League.

Michigan, State of. *Laws Relating to Elections*. 1965.
The "election law" set forth in all its hundreds of sections, which are constantly being revised.

Michigan, State of. *Michigan Manual*.
The yearly guide to almost everything about the men, offices, etc., which make up the Michigan government, including the results of state elections in each locality. This is the first place to look for any information about government in Lansing.

Michigan, State of. *State Constitutions, 1908 and 1962*.
These are available from the office of the secretary of state.

Pealy, Robert H. *Study Kit on Local Government*. Ann Arbor: University of Michigan Press, 1958.
A handy guide to the various forms of city, county, township, and village governments in the state, as well as their judicial and tax systems.

Pealy, Robert H. *The Voter and the Michigan Constitution*. Ann Arbor: University of Michigan Institute of Public Administration, 1960.
A series of essays on several of the major issues in constitutional reform. While many of the issues were decided at the 1961–62 constitutional convention, the book remains instructive in displaying points of view on them.

Pollock, James K. *Making Michigan's Constitution 1961–1962*. Ann Arbor: George Wahr Publishing Company, 1962.
A collection of lectures, given at the University of Michigan during the summer of 1962, concerning the processes and results of the constitutional convention, by one of its most important delegates.

Sturm, Albert L. *Constitution-Making in Michigan, 1961–1962*. Ann Arbor: University of Michigan Institute of Public Administration, 1963.
A detailed account of the events leading to the convention, and the convention itself.

Sawyer, Robert L. *The Democratic State Central Committee in Michigan, 1949 to 1959: The Rise of the New Political Leadership*. Ann Arbor: University of Michigan Institute of Public Administration, 1960.
The story of the amazing rise to power of the Democratic party under the leadership of G. Mennen Williams and the direction of Neil Staebler.

Williams, G. Mennen. *A Governor's Notes*. University of Michigan Institute of Public Administration, 1961.
An intimate look at the political and human aspects of the governorship by the man who served in that office for a record six terms.

CONSTITUTION OF THE STATE OF MICHIGAN

as finally adopted by the Convention August 1, 1962

PREAMBLE

We, the people of the State of Michigan, grateful to Almighty God for the blessings of freedom, and earnestly desiring to secure these blessings undiminished to ourselves and our posterity, do ordain and establish this constitution.

ARTICLE I

Declaration of Rights

Sec. 1. All political power is inherent in the people. Government is instituted for their equal benefit, security and protection.

Sec. 2. No person shall be denied the equal protection of the laws; nor shall any person be denied the enjoyment of his civil or political rights or be discriminated against in the exercise thereof because of religion, race, color or national origin. The legislature shall implement this section by appropriate legislation.

Sec. 3. The people have the right peaceably to assemble, to consult for the common good, to instruct their representatives and to petition the government for redress of grievances.

Sec. 4. Every person shall be at liberty to worship God according to the dictates of his own conscience. No person shall be compelled to attend, or, against his consent, to contribute to the erection or support of any place of religious worship, or to pay tithes, taxes or other rates for the support of any minister of the gospel or teacher of religion. No money shall be appropriated or drawn from the treasury for the benefit of any religious sect or society, theological or religious seminary; nor shall property belonging to the state be appropriated for any such purpose. The civil and political rights, privileges and capacities of no person shall be diminished or enlarged on account of his religious belief.

Sec. 5. Every person may freely speak, write, express and publish his views on all subjects, being responsible for the abuse of such right; and no law shall be enacted to restrain or abridge the liberty of speech or of the press.

Sec. 6. Every person has a right to keep and bear arms for the defense of himself and the state.

Sec. 7. The military shall in all cases and at all times be in strict subordination to the civil power.

Sec. 8. No soldier shall, in time of peace, be quartered in any house without the consent of the owner or occupant, nor in time of war, except in a manner prescribed by law.

Sec. 9. Neither slavery, nor involuntary servitude unless for the punishment of crime, shall ever be tolerated in this state.

Sec. 10. No bill of attainder, ex post facto law or law impairing the obligation of contract shall be enacted.

Sec. 11. The person, houses, papers and possessions of every person shall be secure from unreasonable searches and seizures. No warrant to search any place or to seize any person or things shall issue without describing them, nor without probable cause, supported by oath or affirmation. The provisions of this section shall not be construed to bar from evidence in any criminal proceeding any narcotic drug, firearm, bomb, explosive or any other dangerous weapon, seized by a peace officer outside the curtilage of any dwelling house in this state.

Sec. 12. The privilege of the writ of habeas corpus shall not be suspended unless in case of rebellion or invasion the public safety may require it.

Sec. 13. A suitor in any court of this state has the right to prosecute or defend his suit, either in his own proper person or by an attorney.

Sec. 14. The right of trial by jury shall remain, but shall be waived in all civil cases unless demanded by one of the parties in the manner prescribed by law. In all civil cases tried by 12 jurors a verdict shall be received when 10 jurors agree.

Sec. 15. No person shall be subject for the same offense to be twice put in jeopardy. All persons shall, before conviction, be bailable by sufficient sureties, except for murder and treason when the proof is evident or the presumption great.

Sec. 16. Excessive bail shall not be required; excessive fines shall not be imposed; cruel or unusual punishment shall not be inflicted; nor shall witnesses be unreasonably detained.

Sec. 17. No person shall be compelled in any criminal case to be a witness against himself, nor be deprived of life, liberty or property, without due process of law. The right of all individuals, firms, corporations and voluntary associations to fair and just treatment in the course of legislative and executive investigations and hearings shall not be infringed.

Sec. 18. No person shall be rendered incompetent to be a witness on account of his opinions on matters of religious belief.

Sec. 19. In all prosecutions for libels the truth may be given in evidence to the jury; and, if it appears to the jury that the matter charged as libelous is true and was published with good motives and for justifiable ends, the accused shall be acquitted.

Sec. 20. In every criminal prosecution, the accused shall have the right to a speedy and public trial by an impartial jury, which may consist of less than 12 jurors in all courts not of record; to be informed of the nature of the accusation; to be confronted with the witnesses against him; to have compulsory process for obtaining witnesses in his favor; to have the assistance of counsel for his defense; to have an appeal as a matter of right; and in courts of record, when the trial court so orders, to have such reasonable assistance as may be necessary to perfect and prosecute an appeal.

Sec. 21. No person shall be imprisoned for debt arising out of or founded on contract, express or implied, except in cases of fraud or breach of trust.

Sec. 22. Treason against the state shall consist only in levying war against it or in adhering to its enemies, giving them aid and comfort. No person shall be convicted of treason unless upon the testimony of two witnesses to the same overt act or on confession in open court.

Sec. 23. The enumeration in this constitution of certain rights shall not be construed to deny or disparage others retained by the people.

ARTICLE II

Elections

Sec. 1. Every citizen of the United States who has attained the age of 21 years, who has resided in this state six months, and who meets the requirements of local residence provided by law, shall be an elector and qualified to vote in any election except as otherwise provided in this constitution. The legislature shall define residence for voting purposes.

Sec. 2. The legislature may by law exclude persons from voting because of mental incompetence or commitment to a jail or penal institution.

Sec. 3. For purposes of voting in the election for president and vice-president of the United States only, the legislature may by law establish lesser residence requirements for citizens who have resided in this state for less than six months and may waive residence requirements for former citizens of this state who have removed herefrom. The legislature shall not permit voting by any person who meets the voting residence requirements of the state to which he has removed.

Sec. 4. The legislature shall enact laws to regulate the time, place and manner of all nominations and elections, except as otherwise provided in this constitution or in the constitution and laws of the United States. The legislature shall enact laws to preserve the purity of elections, to preserve the secrecy of the ballot, to guard against abuses of the elective franchise, and to provide for a system of voter registration and absentee voting. No law shall be enacted which permits a candidate in any partisan primary or partisan election to have a ballot designation except when required for identification of candidates for the same office who have the same or similar surnames.

Sec. 5. Except for special elections to fill vacancies, or as otherwise provided in this constitution, all elections for national, state, county and township offices shall be held on the first Tuesday after the first Monday in November in each even-numbered year or on such other date as members of the congress of the United States are regularly elected.

Sec. 6. Whenever any question is required to be submitted by a political subdivision to the electors for the increase of the ad valorem tax rate limitation imposed by Section 6 of Article IX for a period of more than five years, or for the issue of bonds, only electors in, and who have property assessed for any ad valorem taxes in, any part of the district or territory to be affected by the result of such election or electors who are the lawful husbands or wives of such persons shall be entitled to vote thereon. All electors in the district or territory affected may vote on all other questions.

Sec. 7. A board of state canvassers of four members shall be established by law. No candidate for an office to be canvassed nor any inspector of elections shall be eligible to serve as a member of a board of canvassers. A majority of any board of canvassers shall not be composed of members of the same political party.

Sec. 8. Laws shall be enacted to provide for the recall of all elective officers except judges of courts of record upon petition of electors equal in number to 25 percent of the number of persons voting in the last preceding election for the office of governor in the electoral district of the officer sought to be recalled. The sufficiency of any statement of reasons or grounds procedurally required shall be a political rather than a judicial question.

Sec. 9. The people reserve to themselves the power to propose laws and to enact and reject laws, called the initiative, and the power to approve or reject laws enacted by the legislature, called the referendum. The power of initiative extends only to laws which the legislature may enact under this constitution. The power of referendum does not extend to acts making appropriations for state institutions or to meet deficiencies in state funds and must be invoked in the manner prescribed by law within 90 days following the final adjournment of the legislative session at which the law was enacted. To invoke the initiative or referendum, petitions signed by a number of registered electors, not less than eight percent for initiative and five percent for referendum of the total vote cast for all candidates for governor at the last preceding general election at which a governor was elected shall be required.

No law as to which the power of referendum properly has been invoked shall be effective thereafter unless approved by a majority of the electors voting thereon at the next general election.

Any law proposed by initiative petition shall be either enacted or rejected by the legislature without change or amendment within 40 session days from the time such petition is received by the legislature. If any law proposed by such petition shall be enacted by the legislature it shall be subject to referendum, as hereinafter provided.

If the law so proposed is not enacted by the legislature within the 40 days, the state officer authorized by law shall submit such proposed law to the people for approval or rejection at the next general election. The legislature may reject any measure so proposed by initiative petition and propose a different measure upon the same subject by a yea and nay vote upon separate roll calls, and in such event both measures shall be submitted by such state officer to the electors for approval or rejection at the next general election.

Any law submitted to the people by either initiative or referendum petition and approved by a majority of the votes cast thereon at any election shall take effect 10 days after the date of the official declaration of the vote. No law initiated or adopted by the people shall be subject to the veto power of the governor, and no law adopted by the people at the polls under the initiative provisions of this section shall be amended or repealed, except by a vote of the electors unless otherwise provided in the initiative measure or by three-fourths of the members elected to and serving in each house of the legislature. Laws approved by the people under the referendum provision of this section may be amended by the legislature at any subsequent session thereof. If two or more measures approved by the electors at the same election conflict, that receiving the highest affirmative vote shall prevail.

The legislature shall implement the provisions of this section.

ARTICLE III

General Government

Sec. 1. The seat of government shall be at Lansing.

Sec. 2. The powers of government are divided into three branches: legislative, executive and judicial. No person exercising powers of one branch shall exercise powers properly belonging to another branch except as expressly provided in this constitution.

Sec. 3. There shall be a great seal of the State of Michigan and its use shall be provided by law.

Sec. 4. The militia shall be organized, equipped and disciplined as provided by law.

Sec. 5. Subject to provisions of general law, this state or any political subdivision thereof, any governmental authority or any combination thereof may enter into agreements for the performance, financing or execution of their respective functions, with any one or more of the other states, the United States, the Dominion of Canada, or any political subdivision thereof unless otherwise provided in this constitution. Any other provision of this constitution notwithstanding, an officer or employee of the state or of any such unit of government or subdivision or agency thereof may serve on or with any governmental body established for the purposes set forth in this section and shall not be required to relinquish his office or employment by reason of such service. The legislature may impose such restrictions, limitations or conditions on such service as it may deem appropriate.

Sec. 6. The state shall not be a party to, nor be financially interested in, any work of internal improvement, nor engage in carrying on any such work, except for public internal improvements provided by law.

Sec. 7. The common law and the statute laws now in force, not repugnant to this constitution, shall remain in force until they expire by their own limitations, or are changed, amended or repealed.

Sec. 8. Either house of the legislature or the governor may request the opinion of the supreme court on important questions of law upon solemn occasions as to the constitutionality of legislation after it has been enacted into law but before its effective date.

ARTICLE IV

Legislative Branch

Sec. 1. The legislative power of the State of Michigan is vested in a senate and a house of representatives.

Sec. 2. The senate shall consist of 38 members to be elected from single member districts at the same election as the governor for four-year terms concurrent with the term of office of the governor.

In districting the state for the purpose of electing senators after the official publication of the total population count of each federal decennial census, each county shall be assigned apportionment factors equal to the sum of its percentage of the state's population as shown by the last regular federal decennial census computed to the nearest one-one hundredth of one percent multiplied by four and its percentage of the state's land area computed to the nearest one-one hundredth of one percent.

In arranging the state into senatorial districts, the apportionment commission shall be governed by the following rules:

(1) Counties with 13 or more apportionment factors shall be entitled as a class to senators in the proportion that the total apportionment factors of such counties bear to the total apportionment factors of the state computed to the nearest whole number. After each such county has been allocated one senator, the remaining senators to which this class of counties is entitled shall be distributed among such counties by the method of equal proportions applied to the apportionment factors.

(2) Counties having less than 13 apportionment factors shall be entitled as a class to senators in the proportion that the total apportionment factors of such counties bear to the total apportionment factors of the state computed to the nearest whole number. Such counties shall thereafter be arranged into senatorial districts that are compact, convenient, and contiguous by land, as rectangular in shape as possible, and having as nearly as possible 13 apportionment factors, but in no event less than 10 or more than 16. Insofar as possible, existing senatorial districts at the time of reapportionment shall not be altered unless there is a failure to comply with the above standards.

(3) Counties entitled to two or more senators shall be divided into single member districts. The population of such districts shall be as nearly equal as possible but shall not be less than 75 percent nor more than 125 percent of a number determined by dividing the population of the county by the number of senators to which it is entitled. Each such district shall follow incorporated city or township boundary lines to the extent possible and shall be compact, contiguous, and as nearly uniform in shape as possible.

Sec. 3. The house of representatives shall consist of 110 members elected for two-year terms from single member districts apportioned on a basis of population as provided in this article. The districts shall consist of compact and convenient territory contiguous by land.

Each county which has a population of not less than seven-tenths of one percent of the population of the state shall constitute a separate representative area. Each county having less than seven-tenths of one percent of the population of the state shall be combined with another county or counties to form a representative area of not less than seven-tenths of one percent of the population of the state. Any county which is isolated under the initial allocation as provided in this section shall be joined with that contiguous representative area having the smallest percentage of the state's population. Each such representative area shall be entitled initially to one representative.

After the assignment of one representative to each of the representative areas, the remaining house seats shall be apportioned among the representative areas on the basis of population by the method of equal proportions.

Any county comprising a representative area entitled to two or more representatives shall be divided into single member representative districts as follows:

(1) The population of such districts shall be as nearly equal as possible but shall not be less than 75 percent nor more than 125 percent of a number determined by dividing the population of the representative area by the number of representatives to which it is entitled.

(2) Such single member districts shall follow city and township boundaries where applicable and shall be composed of compact and contiguous territory as nearly square in shape as possible.

Any representative area consisting of more than one county, entitled to more than one representative, shall be divided into single member districts as equal as possible in population, adhering to county lines.

Sec. 4. In counties having more than one representative or senatorial district, the territory in the same county annexed to or merged with a city between apportionments shall become a part of a contiguous representative or senatorial district in the city with which it is combined, if provided by ordinance of the city. The district or districts with which the territory shall be combined shall be determined by such ordinance certified to the secretary of state. No such change in the boundaries of a representative or senatorial district shall have the effect of removing a legislator from office during his term.

Sec. 5. Island areas are considered to be contiguous by land to the county of which they are a part.

Sec. 6. A commission on legislative apportionment is hereby established consisting of eight electors, four of whom shall be selected by the state organizations of each of the two political parties whose candidates for governor received the highest vote at the last general election at which a governor was elected preceding each apportionment. If a candidate for governor of a third political party has received at such election more than 25 percent of such gubernatorial vote, the commission shall consist of 12 members, four of whom shall be selected by the state organization of the third political party. One resident of each of the following four regions shall be selected by each political party organization: (1) the upper peninsula; (2) the northern part of the lower peninsula, north of a line drawn along the northern boundaries of the counties of Bay, Midland, Isabella, Mecosta, Newaygo and Oceana; (3) southwestern Michigan, those counties south of region (2) and west of a line drawn along the western boundaries of the counties of Bay, Saginaw, Shiawassee, Ingham, Jackson and Hillsdale; (4) southeastern Michigan, the remaining counties of the state.

No officers or employees of the federal, state or local governments, excepting notaries public and members of the armed forces reserve, shall be eligible for membership on the commission. Members of the commission shall not be eligible for election to the legislature until two years after the apportionment in which they participated becomes effective.

The commission shall be appointed immediately after the adoption of this constitution and whenever apportionment or districting of the legislature is required by the provisions of this constitution. Members of the commission shall hold office until each apportionment or districting plan becomes effective. Vacancies shall be filled in the same manner as for original appointment.

The secretary of state shall be secretary of the commission without vote, and in that capacity shall furnish, under the direction of the commission, all necessary technical services. The commission shall elect its own chairman, shall make its own rules of procedure, and shall receive compensation provided by law. The legislature shall appropriate funds to enable the commission to carry out its activities.

Within 30 days after the adoption of this constitution, and after the official total population count of each federal decennial census of the state and its political subdivisions is available, the secretary of state shall issue a call convening the commission not less than 30 nor more than 45 days thereafter. The commission shall complete its work within 180 days after all necessary census information is available. The commission shall proceed to district and apportion the senate and house of representatives according to the provisions of this constitution. All final decisions shall require the concurrence of a majority of the members of the commission. The commission shall hold public hearings as may be provided by law.

Each final apportionment and districting plan shall be published as provided by law within 30 days from the date of its adoption and shall become law 60 days after publication. The secretary of state shall keep a public record of all the proceedings of the commission and shall be responsible for the publication and distribution of each plan.

If a majority of the commission cannot agree on a plan, each member of the commission, individually or jointly with other members, may submit a proposed plan to the supreme court. The supreme court shall determine which plan complies most accurately with the constitutional requirements and shall direct that it be adopted by the commission and published as provided in this section.

Upon the application of any elector filed not later than 60 days after final publication of the plan, the supreme court, in the exercise of original jurisdiction, shall direct the secretary of state or the commission to perform their duties, may review any final plan adopted by the commission, and shall remand such plan to the commission for further action if it fails to comply with the requirements of this constitution.

Sec. 7. Each senator and representative must be a citizen of the United States, at least 21 years of age, and an elector of the district he represents. The removal of his domicile from the district shall be deemed a vacation of the office. No person who has been convicted of subversion or who has within the preceding 20 years been convicted of a felony involving a breach of public trust shall be eligible for either house of the legislature.

Sec. 8. No person holding any office, employment or position under the United States or this state or a political subdivision thereof, except notaries public and members of the armed forces reserve, may be a member of either house of the legislature.

Sec. 9. No person elected to the legislature shall receive any civil appointment within this state from the governor, except notaries public, from the legislature, or from any other state authority, during the term for which he is elected.

Sec. 10. No member of the legislature nor any state officer shall be interested directly or indirectly in any contract with the state or any political subdivision thereof which shall cause a substantial conflict of interest. The legislature shall further implement this provision by appropriate legislation.

Sec. 11. Senators and representatives shall be privileged from civil arrest and civil process during sessions of the legislature and for five days next before the commencement and after the termination thereof. They shall not be questioned in any other place for any speech in either house.

Sec. 12. The compensation and expense allowances of the members of the legislature shall be determined by law. Changes in compensation or expense allowances shall become effective only when legislators commence their terms of office after a general election.

Sec. 13. The legislature shall meet at the seat of government on the second Wednesday in January of each year at twelve o'clock noon. Each regular session shall adjourn without day, on a day determined by concurrent resolution, at twelve o'clock noon. Any business, bill or joint resolution pending at the final adjournment of a regular session held in an odd numbered year shall carry over with the same status to the next regular session.

Sec. 14. A majority of the members elected to and serving in each house shall constitute a quorum to do business. A smaller number in each house may adjourn from day to day, and may compel the attendance of absent members in the manner and with penalties as each house may prescribe.

Sec. 15. There shall be a bi-partisan legislative council consisting of legislators appointed in the manner prescribed by law. The legislature shall appropriate funds for the council's operations and provide for its staff which shall maintain bill drafting, research and other services for the members of the legislature. The council shall periodically examine and recommend to the legislature revision of the various laws of the state.

Sec. 16. Each house, except as otherwise provided in this constitution, shall choose its own officers and determine the rules of its proceedings, but shall not adopt any rule that will prevent a majority of the members elected thereto and serving therein from discharging a committee from the further consideration of any measure. Each house shall be the sole judge of the qualifications, elections and returns of its members, and may, with the concurrence of two-thirds of all the members elected thereto and serving therein, expel a member. The reasons for such expulsion shall be entered in the journal, with the votes and names of the members voting upon the question. No member shall be expelled a second time for the same cause.

Sec. 17. Each house of the legislature may establish the committees necessary for the efficient conduct of its business and the legislature may create joint committees. On all actions on bills and resolutions in each committee, names and votes of members shall be recorded. Such vote shall be available for public inspection. Notice of all committee hearings and a clear statement of all subjects to be considered at each hearing shall be published in the journal in advance of the hearing.

Sec. 18. Each house shall keep a journal of its proceedings, and publish the same unless the public security otherwise requires. The record of the vote and name of the members of either house voting on any question shall be entered in the journal at the request of one-fifth of the members present. Any member of either house may dissent from and protest against any act, proceeding or resolution which he deems injurious to any person or the public, and have the reason for his dissent entered in the journal.

Sec. 19. All elections in either house or in joint convention and all votes on appointments submitted to the senate for advice and consent shall be published by vote and name in the journal.

Sec. 20. The doors of each house shall be open unless the public security otherwise requires.

Sec. 21. Neither house shall, without the consent of the other, adjourn for more than two intervening calendar days, nor to any place other than where the legislature may then be in session.

Sec. 22. All legislation shall be by bill and may originate in either house.

Sec. 23. The style of the laws shall be: The People of the State of Michigan enact.

Sec. 24. No law shall embrace more than one object, which shall be expressed in its title. No bill shall be altered or amended on its passage through either house so as to change its original purpose as determined by its total content and not alone by its title.

Sec. 25. No law shall be revised, altered or amended by reference to its title only. The section or sections of the act altered or amended shall be re-enacted and published at length.

Sec. 26. No bill shall be passed or become a law at any regular session of the legislature until it has been printed or reproduced and in the possession of each house for at least five days. Every bill shall be read three times in each house before the final passage thereof. No bill shall become a law without the concurrence of a majority of the members elected to and serving in each house. On the final passage of bills, the votes and names of the members voting thereon shall be entered in the journal.

Sec. 27. No act shall take effect until the expiration of 90 days from the end of the session at which it was passed, but the legislature may give immediate effect to acts by a two-thirds vote of the members elected to and serving in each house.

Sec. 28. When the legislature is convened on extraordinary occasions in special session no bill shall be passed on any subjects other than those expressly stated in the governor's proclamation or submitted by special message.

Sec. 29. The legislature shall pass no local or special act in any case where a general act can be made applicable, and whether a general act can be made applicable shall be a judicial question. No local or special act shall take effect until approved by two-thirds of the members elected to and serving in each house and by a majority of the electors voting thereon in the district affected. Any act repealing local or special acts shall require only a majority of the members elected to and serving in each house and shall not require submission to the electors of such district.

Sec. 30. The assent of two-thirds of the members elected to and serving in each house of the legislature shall be required for the appropriation of public money or property for local or private purposes.

Sec. 31. The general appropriation bills for the succeeding fiscal period covering items set forth in the budget shall be passed or rejected in either house of the legislature before that house passes any appropriation bill for items not in the budget except bills supplementing appropriations for the current fiscal year's operation. Any bill requiring an appropriation to carry out its purpose shall be considered an appropriation bill. One of the general appropriation bills as passed by the legislature shall contain an itemized statement of estimated revenue by major source in each operating fund for the ensuing fiscal period, the total of which shall not be less than the total of all appropriations made from each fund in the general appropriation bills as passed.

Sec. 32. Every law which imposes, continues or revives a tax shall distinctly state the tax.

Sec. 33. Every bill passed by the legislature shall be presented to the governor before it becomes law, and the governor shall have 14 days measured in hours and minutes from the time of presentation in which to consider it. If he approves, he shall within that time sign and file it with the secretary of state and it shall become law. If he does not approve, and the legislature has within that time finally adjourned the session at which the bill was passed, it shall not become law. If he disapproves, and the legislature continues the session at which the bill was passed, he shall return it within such 14-day period with his objections, to the house in which it originated. That house shall enter such objections in full in its journal and reconsider the bill. If two-thirds of the members elected to and serving in that house pass the bill notwithstanding the objections of the governor, it shall be sent with the objections to the other house for reconsideration. The bill shall become law if passed by two-thirds of the members elected to and serving in that house. The vote of each house shall be entered in the journal with the votes and names of the members voting thereon. If any bill is not returned by the governor within such 14-day period, the legislature continuing in session, it shall become law as if he had signed it.

Sec. 34. Any bill passed by the legislature and approved by the governor, except a bill appropriating money, may provide that it will not become law unless approved by a majority of the electors voting thereon.

Sec. 35. All laws enacted at any session of the legislature shall be published in book form within 60 days after final adjournment of the session, and shall be distributed in the manner provided by law. The prompt publication of judicial decisions shall be provided by law. All laws and judicial decisions shall be free for publication by any person.

Sec. 36. No general revision of the laws shall be made. The legislature may provide for a compilation of the laws in force, arranged without alteration, under appropriate heads and titles.

Sec. 37. The legislature may by concurrent resolution empower a joint committee of the legislature, acting between sessions, to suspend any rule or regulation promulgated by an administrative agency subsequent to the adjournment of the last preceding regular legislative session. Such suspension shall continue no longer than the end of the next regular legislative session.

Sec. 38. The legislature may provide by law the cases in which any office shall be vacant and the manner of filling vacancies where no provision is made in this constitution.

Sec. 39. In order to insure continuity of state and local governmental operations in periods of emergency only, resulting from disasters occurring in this state caused by enemy attack on the United States, the legislature may provide by law for prompt and temporary succession to the powers and duties of public offices, of whatever nature and whether filled by election or appointment, the incumbents of which may become unavailable for carrying on the powers and duties of such offices; and enact other laws necessary and proper for insuring the continuity of governmental operations. Notwithstanding the power conferred by this section, elections shall always be called as soon as possible to fill any vacancies in elective offices temporarily occupied by operation of any legislation enacted pursuant to the provisions of this section.

Sec. 40. The legislature may by law establish a liquor control commission which, subject to statutory limitations, shall exercise complete control of the alcoholic beverage traffic within this state, including the retail sales thereof. The legislature may provide for an excise tax on such sales. Neither the legislature nor the commission may authorize the manufacture or sale of alcoholic beverages in any county in which a majority of the electors voting thereon shall prohibit the same.

Sec. 41. The legislature shall not authorize any lottery nor permit the sale of lottery tickets.

Sec. 42. The legislature may provide for the incorporation of ports and port districts, and confer power and authority upon them to engage in work of internal improvements in connection therewith.

Sec. 43. No general law providing for the incorporation of trust companies or corporations for banking purposes, or regulating the business thereof, shall be enacted, amended or repealed except by a vote of two-thirds of the members elected to and serving in each house.

Sec. 44. The legislature may authorize a trial by a jury of less than 12 jurors in civil cases.

Sec. 45. The legislature may provide for indeterminate sentences as punishment for crime and for the detention and release of persons imprisoned or detained under such sentences.

Sec. 46. No law shall be enacted providing for the penalty of death.

Sec. 47. The legislature may authorize the employment of chaplains in state institutions of detention or confinement.

Sec. 48. The legislature may enact laws providing for the resolution of disputes concerning public employees, except those in the state classified civil service.

Sec. 49. The legislature may enact laws relative to the hours and conditions of employment.

Sec. 50. The legislature may provide safety measures and regulate the use of atomic energy and forms of energy developed in the future, having in view the general welfare of the people of this state.

Sec. 51. The public health and general welfare of the people of the state are hereby declared to be matters of primary public concern. The legislature shall pass suitable laws for the protection and promotion of the public health.

Sec. 52. The conservation and development of the natural resources of the state are hereby declared to be of paramount public concern in the interest of the health, safety and general welfare of the people. The legislature shall provide for the protection of the air, water and other natural resources of the state from pollution, impairment and destruction.

Sec. 53. The legislature by a majority vote of the members elected to and serving in each house, shall appoint an auditor general, who shall be a certified public accountant licensed to practice in this state, to serve for a term of eight years. He shall be ineligible for appointment or election to any other public office in this state from which compensation is derived while serving as auditor general and for two years following the termination of his service. He may be removed for cause at any time by a two-thirds vote of the members elected to and serving in each house. The auditor general shall conduct post audits of financial transactions and accounts of the state and of all branches, departments, offices, boards, commissions, agencies, authorities and institutions of the state established by this constitution or by law, and performance post audits thereof.

The auditor general upon direction by the legislature may employ independent accounting firms or legal counsel and may make investigations pertinent to the conduct of audits. He shall report annually to the legislature and to the governor and at such other times as he deems necessary or as required by the legislature. He shall be assigned no duties other than those specified in this section.

Nothing in this section shall be construed in any way to infringe the responsibility and constitutional authority of the governing boards of the institutions of higher education to be solely responsible for the control and direction of all expenditures from the institutions' funds.

The auditor general, his deputy and one other member of his staff shall be exempt from classified civil service. All other members of his staff shall have classified civil service status.

ARTICLE V

Executive Branch

Sec. 1. The executive power is vested in the governor.

Sec. 2. All executive and administrative offices, agencies and instrumentalities of the executive branch of state government and their respective functions, powers and duties, except for the office of governor and lieutenant governor and the governing bodies of institutions of higher education provided for in this constitution, shall be allocated by law among and within not more than 20 principal departments. They shall be grouped as far as practicable according to major purposes.

Subsequent to the initial allocation, the governor may make changes in the organization of the executive branch or in the assignment of functions among its units which he considers necessary for efficient administration. Where these changes require the force of law, they shall be set forth in executive orders and submitted to the legislature. Thereafter the legislature shall have 60 calendar days of a regular session, or a full regular session if of shorter duration, to disapprove each executive order. Unless disapproved in both houses by a resolution concurred in by a majority of the members elected to and serving in each house, each order shall become effective at a date thereafter to be designated by the governor.

Sec. 3. The head of each principal department shall be a single executive unless otherwise provided in this constitution or by law. The single executives heading principal departments shall include a secretary of state, a state treasurer and an attorney general. When a single executive is the head of a principal department, unless elected or appointed as otherwise provided in this constitution, he shall be appointed by the governor by and with the advice and consent of the senate and he shall serve at the pleasure of the governor.

When a board or commission is at the head of a principal department, unless elected or appointed as otherwise provided in this constitution, the members thereof shall be appointed by the governor by and with the advice and consent of the senate. The term of office and procedure for removal of such members shall be as prescribed in this constitution or by law.

Terms of office of any board or commission created or enlarged after the effective date of this constitution shall not exceed four years except as otherwise authorized in this constitution. The terms of office of existing boards and commissions which are longer than four years shall not be further extended except as provided in this constitution.

Sec. 4. Temporary commissions or agencies for special purposes with a life of no more than two years may be established by law and need not be allocated within a principal department.

Sec. 5. A majority of the members of an appointed examining or licensing board of a profession shall be members of that profession.

Sec. 6. Appointment by and with the advice and consent of the senate when used in this constitution or laws in effect or hereafter enacted means appointment subject to disapproval by a majority vote of the members elected to and serving in the senate if such action is taken within 60 session days after the date of such appointment. Any appointment not disapproved within such period shall stand confirmed.

Sec. 7. Vacancies in any office, appointment to which requires advice and consent of the senate, shall be filled by the governor by and with the advice and consent of the senate. A person whose appointment has been disapproved by the senate shall not be eligible for an interim appointment to the same office.

Sec. 8. Each principal department shall be under the supervision of the governor unless otherwise provided by this constitution. The governor shall take care that the laws be faithfully executed. He shall transact all necessary business with the officers of government and may require information in writing from all executive and administrative state officers, elective and appointive, upon any subject relating to the duties of their respective offices.

The governor may initiate court proceedings in the name of the state to enforce compliance with any constitutional or legislative mandate, or to restrain violations of any constitutional or legislative power, duty or right by any officer, department or agency of the state or any of its political subdivisions. This authority shall not be construed to authorize court proceedings against the legislature.

Sec. 9. Single executives heading principal departments and the chief executive officers of principal departments headed by boards or commissions shall keep their offices at the seat of government except as otherwise provided by law, superintend them in person and perform duties prescribed by law.

Sec. 10. The governor shall have power and it shall be his duty to inquire into the condition and administration of any public office and the acts of any public officer, elective or appointive. He may remove or suspend from office for gross neglect of duty or for corrupt conduct in office, or for any other misfeasance or malfeasance therein, any elective or appointive state officer, except legislative or judicial, and shall report the reasons for such removal or suspension to the legislature.

Sec. 11. The governor may make a provisional appointment to fill a vacancy occasioned by the suspension of an appointed or elected officer, other than a legislative or judicial officer, until he is reinstated or until the vacancy is filled in the manner prescribed by law or this constitution.

Sec. 12. The governor shall be commander-in-chief of the armed forces and may call them out to execute the laws, suppress insurrection and repel invasion.

Sec. 13. The governor shall issue writs of election to fill vacancies in the senate or house of representatives. Any such election shall be held in a manner prescribed by law.

Sec. 14. The governor shall have power to grant reprieves, commutations and pardons after convictions for all offenses, except cases of impeachment, upon such conditions and limitations as he may direct, subject to procedures and regulations prescribed by law. He shall inform the legislature annually of each reprieve, commutation and pardon granted, stating reasons therefor.

Sec. 15. The governor may convene the legislature on extraordinary occasions.

Sec. 16. The governor may convene the legislature at some other place when the seat of government becomes dangerous from any cause.

Sec. 17. The governor shall communicate by message to the legislature at the beginning of each session and may at other times present to the legislature information as to the affairs of the state and recommend measures he considers necessary or desirable.

Sec. 18. The governor shall submit to the legislature at a time fixed by law, a budget for the ensuing fiscal period setting forth in detail, for all operating funds, the proposed expenditures and estimated revenue of the state. Proposed expenditures from any fund shall not exceed the estimated revenue thereof. On the same date, the governor shall submit to the legislature general appropriation bills to embody the proposed expenditures and any necessary bill or bills to provide new or additional revenues to meet proposed expenditures. The amount of any surplus created or deficit incurred in any fund during the last preceding fiscal period shall be entered as an item in the budget and in one of the appropriation bills. The governor may submit amendments to appropriation bills to be offered in either house during consideration of the bill by that house, and shall submit bills to meet deficiencies in current appropriations.

Sec. 19. The governor may disapprove any distinct item or items appropriating moneys in any appropriation bill. The part or parts approved shall become law, and the item or items disapproved shall be void unless re-passed according to the method prescribed for the passage of other bills over the executive veto.

Sec. 20. No appropriation shall be a mandate to spend. The governor, with the approval of the appropriating committees of the house and senate, shall reduce expenditures authorized by appropriations whenever it appears that actual revenues for a fiscal period will fall below the revenue estimates on which appropriations for that period were based. Reductions in expenditures shall be made in accordance with procedures prescribed by law. The governor may not reduce expenditures of the legislative and judicial branches or from funds constitutionally dedicated for specific purposes.

Sec. 21. The governor, lieutenant governor, secretary of state and attorney general shall be elected for four-year terms at the general election in each alternate even-numbered year.

The lieutenant governor, secretary of state and attorney general shall be nominated by party conventions in a manner prescribed by law. In the general election one vote shall be cast jointly for the candidates for governor and lieutenant governor nominated by the same party.

Vacancies in the office of the secretary of state and attorney general shall be filled by appointment by the governor.

Sec. 22. To be eligible for the office of governor or lieutenant governor a person must have attained the age of 30 years, and have been a registered elector in this state for four years next preceding his election.

Sec. 23. The governor, lieutenant governor, secretary of state and attorney general shall each receive the compensation provided by law in full payment for all services performed and expenses incurred during his term of office. Such compensation shall not be changed during the term of office except as otherwise provided in this constitution.

Sec. 24. An executive residence suitably furnished shall be provided at the seat of government for the use of the governor. He shall receive an allowance for its maintenance as provided by law.

Sec. 25. The lieutenant governor shall be president of the senate, but shall have no vote, unless they be equally divided. He may perform duties requested of him by the governor, but no power vested in the governor shall be delegated.

Sec. 26. In case of the conviction of the governor on impeachment, his removal from office, his resignation or his death, the lieutenant governor, the elected secretary of state, the elected attorney general and such other persons designated by law shall in that order be governor for the remainder of the governor's term.

In case of the death of the governor-elect, the lieutenant governor-elect, the secretary of state-elect, the attorney general-elect and such other persons designated by law shall become governor in that order at the commencement of the governor-elect's term.

If the governor or the person in line of succession to serve as governor is absent from the state, or suffering under an inability, the powers and duties of the office of governor shall devolve in order of precedence until the absence or inability giving rise to the devolution of powers ceases.

The inability of the governor or person acting as governor shall be determined by a majority of the supreme court on joint request of the president pro tempore of the senate and the speaker of the house of representatives. Such determination shall be final and conclusive. The supreme court shall upon its own initiative determine if and when the inability ceases.

Sec. 27. The legislature shall provide that the salary of any state officer while acting as governor shall be equal to that of the governor.

Sec. 28. There is hereby established a state highway commission, which shall administer the state highway department and have jurisdiction and control over all state trunkline highways and appurtenant facilities, and such other public works of the state, as provided by law.

The state highway commission shall consist of four members, not more than two of whom shall be members of the same political party. They shall be appointed by the governor by and with the advice and consent of the senate for four-year terms, no two of which shall expire in the same year, as provided by law.

The state highway commission shall appoint and may remove a state highway director, who shall be a competent highway engineer and administrator. He shall be the principal executive officer of the state highway department and shall be responsible for executing the policy of the state highway commission.

Sec. 29. There is hereby established a civil rights commission which shall consist of eight persons, not more than four of whom shall be members of the same political party, who shall be appointed by the governor, by and with the advice and consent of the senate, for four-year terms not more than two of which shall expire in the same year. It shall be the duty of the commission in a manner which may be prescribed by law to investigate alleged discrimination against any person because of religion, race, color or national origin in the enjoyment of the civil rights guaranteed by law and by this constitution, and to secure the equal protection of such civil rights without such discrimination. The legislature shall provide an annual appropriation for the effective operation of the commission.

The commission shall have power, in accordance with the provisions of this constitution and of general laws governing administrative agencies, to promulgate rules and regulations for its own procedures, to hold hearings, administer oaths, through court authorization to require the attendance of witnesses and the submission of records, to take testimony, and to issue appropriate orders. The commission shall have other powers provided by law to carry out its purposes. Nothing contained in this section shall be construed to diminish the right of any party to direct and immediate legal or equitable remedies in the courts of this state.

Appeals from final orders of the commission, including cease and desist orders and refusals to issue complaints, shall be tried de novo before the circuit court having jurisdiction provided by law.

ARTICLE VI

Judicial Branch

Sec. 1. The judicial power of the state is vested exclusively in one court of justice which shall be divided into one supreme court, one court of appeals, one trial court of general jurisdiction known as the circuit court, one probate court, and courts of limited jurisdiction that the legislature may establish by a two-thirds vote of the members elected to and serving in each house.

Sec. 2. The supreme court shall consist of seven justices elected at non-partisan elections as provided by law. The term of office shall be eight years and not more than two terms of office shall expire at the same time. Nominations for justices of the supreme court shall be in the manner prescribed by law. Any incumbent justice whose term is to expire may become a candidate for re-election by filing an affidavit of candidacy, in the form and manner prescribed by law, not less than 180 days prior to the expiration of his term.

Sec. 3. One justice of the supreme court shall be selected by the court as its chief justice as provided by rules of the court. He shall perform duties required by the court. The supreme court shall appoint an administrator of the courts and other assistants of the supreme court as may be necessary to aid in the administration of the courts of this state. The administrator shall perform administrative duties assigned by the court.

Sec. 4. The supreme court shall have general superintending control over all courts; power to issue, hear and determine prerogative and remedial writs; and appellate jurisdiction as provided by rules of the supreme court. The supreme court shall not have the power to remove a judge.

Sec. 5. The supreme court shall by general rules establish, modify, amend and simplify the practice and procedure in all courts of this state. The distinctions between law and equity proceedings shall, as far as practicable, be abolished. The office of master in chancery is prohibited.

Sec. 6. Decisions of the supreme court, including all decisions on prerogative writs, shall be in writing and shall contain a concise statement of the facts and reasons for each decision and reasons for each denial of leave to appeal. When a judge dissents in whole or in part he shall give in writing the reasons for his dissent.

Sec. 7. The supreme court may appoint, may remove, and shall have general supervision of its staff. It shall have control of the preparation of its budget recommendations and the expenditure of moneys appropriated for any purpose pertaining to the operation of the court or the performance of activities of its staff except that the salaries of the justices shall be established by law. All fees and perquisites collected by the court staff shall be turned over to the state treasury and credited to the general fund.

Sec. 8. The court of appeals shall consist initially of nine judges who shall be nominated and elected at non-partisan elections from districts drawn on county lines and as nearly as possible of equal population, as provided by law. The supreme court may prescribe by rule that the court of appeals sit in divisions and for the terms of court and the times and places thereof. Each such division shall consist of not fewer than three judges. The number of judges comprising the court of appeals may be increased, and the districts from which they are elected may be changed by law.

Sec. 9. Judges of the court of appeals shall hold office for a term of six years and until their successors are elected and qualified. The terms of office for the judges in each district shall be arranged by law to provide that not all terms will expire at the same time.

Sec. 10. The jurisdiction of the court of appeals shall be provided by law and the practice and procedure therein shall be prescribed by rules of the supreme court.

Sec. 11. The state shall be divided into judicial circuits along county lines in each of which there shall be elected one or more circuit judges as provided by law. Sessions of the circuit court shall be held at least four times in each year in every county organized for judicial purposes. Each circuit judge shall hold court in the county or counties within the circuit in which he is elected, and in other circuits as may be provided by rules of the supreme court. The number of judges may be changed and circuits may be created, altered and discontinued by law and the number of judges shall be changed and circuits shall be created, altered and discontinued on recommendation of the supreme court to reflect changes in judicial activity. No change in the number of judges or alteration or discontinuance of a circuit shall have the effect of removing a judge from office during his term.

Sec. 12. Circuit judges shall be nominated and elected at non-partisan elections in the circuit in which they reside, and shall hold office for a term of six years and until their successors are elected and qualified. In circuits having more than one circuit judge their terms of office shall be arranged by law to provide that not all terms will expire at the same time.

Sec. 13. The circuit court shall have original jurisdiction in all matters not prohibited by law; appellate jurisdiction from all inferior courts and tribunals except as otherwise provided by law; power to issue, hear and determine prerogative and remedial writs; supervisory and general control over inferior courts and tribunals within their respective jurisdictions in accordance with rules of the supreme court; and jurisdiction of other cases and matters as provided by rules of the supreme court.

Sec. 14. The clerk of each county organized for judicial purposes or other officer performing the duties of such office as provided in a county charter shall be clerk of the circuit court for such county. The judges of the circuit court may fill a vacancy in an elective office of county clerk or prosecuting attorney within their respective jurisdictions.

Sec. 15. In each county organized for judicial purposes there shall be a probate court. The legislature may create or alter probate court districts of more than one county if approved in each affected county by a majority of the electors voting on the question. The legislature may provide for the combination of the office of probate judge with any judicial office of limited jurisdiction within a county with supplemental salary as provided by law. The jurisdiction, powers and duties of the probate court and of the judges thereof shall be provided by law. They shall have original jurisdiction in all cases of juvenile delinquents and dependents, except as otherwise provided by law.

Sec. 16. One or more judges of probate as provided by law shall be nominated and elected at non-partisan elections in the counties or the probate districts in which they reside and shall hold office for terms of six years and until their successors are elected and qualified. In counties or districts with more than one judge the terms of office shall be arranged by law to provide that not all terms will expire at the same time.

Sec. 17. No judge or justice of any court of this state shall be paid from the fees of his office nor shall the amount of his salary be measured by fees, other moneys received or the amount of judicial activity of his office.

Sec. 18 Salaries of justices of the supreme court, of the judges of the court of appeals, of the circuit judges within a circuit, and of the probate judges within a county or district, shall be uniform, and may be increased but shall not be decreased during a term of office except and only to the extent of a general salary reduction in all other branches of government.

Each of the judges of the circuit court shall receive an annual salary as provided by law. In addition to the salary received from the state, each circuit judge may receive from any county in which he regularly holds court an additional salary as determined from time to time by the board of supervisors of the county. In any county where an additional salary is granted, it shall be paid at the same rate to all circuit judges regularly holding court therein.

Sec. 19. The supreme court, the court of appeals, the circuit court, the probate court and other courts designated as such by the legislature shall be courts of record and each shall have a common seal. Justices and judges of courts of record must be persons who are licensed to practice law in this state. No person shall be elected or appointed to a judicial office after reaching the age of 70 years.

Sec. 20. Whenever a justice or judge removes his domicile beyond the limits of the territory from which he was elected, he shall have vacated his office.

Sec. 21. Any justice or judge of a court of record shall be ineligible to be nominated for or elected to an elective office other than a judicial office during the period of his service and for one year thereafter.

Sec. 22. Any elected judge of the court of appeals, circuit court or probate court may become a candidate in the primary election for the office of which he is the incumbent by filing an affidavit of candidacy in the form and manner prescribed by law.

Sec. 23. A vacancy in the elective office of a judge of any court of record shall be filled at a general or special election as provided by law. The supreme court may authorize persons who have served as judges and who have retired, to perform judicial duties for the limited period of time from the occurrence of the vacancy until the successor is elected and qualified. Such persons shall be ineligible for election to fill the vacancy.

Sec. 24. There shall be printed upon the ballot under the name of each elected incumbent justice or judge who is a candidate for nomination or election to the same office the designation of that office.

Sec. 25. For reasonable cause, which is not sufficient ground for impeachment, the governor shall remove any judge on a concurrent resolution of two-thirds of the members elected to and serving in each house of the legislature. The cause for removal shall be stated at length in the resolution.

Sec. 26. The offices of circuit court commissioner and justice of the peace are abolished at the expiration of five years from the date this constitution becomes effective or may within this period be abolished by law. Their jurisdiction, compensation and powers within this period shall be as provided by law. Within this five-year period, the legislature shall establish a court or courts of limited jurisdiction with powers and jurisdiction defined by law. The location of such court or courts, and the qualifications, tenure, method of election and salary of the judges of such court or courts, and by what governmental units the judges shall be paid, shall be provided by law, subject to the limitations contained in this article.

Statutory courts in existence at the time this constitution becomes effective shall retain their powers and jurisdiction, except as provided by law, until they are abolished by law.

Sec. 27. The supreme court, the court of appeals, the circuit court, or any justices or judges thereof, shall not exercise any power of appointment to public office except as provided in this constitution.

Sec. 28. All final decisions, findings, rulings and orders of any administrative officer or agency existing under the constitution or by law, which are judicial or quasi-judicial and affect private rights or licenses, shall be subject to direct review by the courts as provided by law. This review shall include, as a minimum, the determination whether such final decisions, findings, rulings and orders are authorized by law; and, in cases in which a hearing is required, whether the same are supported by competent, material and substantial evidence on the whole record. Findings of fact in workmen's compensation proceedings shall be conclusive in the absence of fraud unless otherwise provided by law.

In the absence of fraud, error of law or the adoption of wrong principles, no appeal may be taken to any court from any final agency provided for the administration of property tax laws from any decision relating to valuation or allocation.

Sec. 29. Justices of the supreme court, judges of the court of appeals, circuit judges and other judges as provided by law shall be conservators of the peace within their respective jurisdictions.

ARTICLE VII
Local Government

Sec. 1. Each organized county shall be a body corporate with powers and immunities provided by law.

Sec. 2. Any county may frame, adopt, amend or repeal a county charter in a manner and with powers and limitations to be provided by general law, which shall among other things provide for the election of a charter commission. The law may permit the organization of county government in form different from that set forth in this constitution and shall limit the rate of ad valorem property taxation for county purposes, and restrict the powers of charter counties to borrow money and contract debts. Each charter county is hereby granted power to levy other taxes for county purposes subject to limitations and prohibitions set forth in this constitution or law. Subject to law, a county charter may authorize the county through its regularly constituted authority to adopt resolutions and ordinances relating to its concerns.

The board of supervisors by a majority vote of its members may, and upon petition of five percent of the electors shall, place upon the ballot the question of electing a commission to frame a charter.

No county charter shall be adopted, amended or repealed until approved by a majority of electors voting on the question.

Sec. 3. No organized county shall be reduced by the organization of new counties to less than 16 townships as surveyed by the United States, unless approved in the manner prescribed by law by a majority of electors voting thereon in each county to be affected.

Sec. 4. There shall be elected for four-year terms in each organized county a sheriff, a county clerk, a county treasurer, a register of deeds and a prosecuting attorney, whose duties and powers shall be provided by law. The board of supervisors in any county may combine the offices of county clerk and register of deeds in one office or separate the same at pleasure.

Sec. 5. The sheriff, county clerk, county treasurer and register of deeds shall hold their principal offices at the county seat.

Sec. 6. The sheriff may be required by law to renew his security periodically and in default of giving such security, his office shall be vacant. The county shall never be responsible for his acts, except that the board of supervisors may protect him against claims by prisoners for unintentional injuries received while in his custody. He shall not hold any other office except in civil defense.

Sec. 7. A board of supervisors shall be established in each organized county consisting of one member from each organized township and such representation from cities as provided by law.

Sec. 8. Boards of supervisors shall have legislative, administrative and such other powers and duties as provided by law.

Sec. 9. Boards of supervisors shall have exclusive power to fix the compensation of county officers not otherwise provided by law.

Sec. 10. A county seat once established shall not be removed until the place to which it is proposed to be moved shall be designated by two-thirds of the members of the board of supervisors and a majority of the electors voting thereon shall have approved the proposed location in the manner prescribed by law.

Sec. 11. No county shall incur any indebtedness which shall increase its total debt beyond 10 percent of its assessed valuation.

Sec. 12. A navigable stream shall not be bridged or dammed without permission granted by the board of supervisors of the county as provided by law, which permission shall be subject to such reasonable compensation and other conditions as may seem best suited to safeguard the rights and interests of the county and political subdivisions therein.

Sec. 13. Two or more contiguous counties may combine into a single county if approved in each affected county by a majority of the electors voting on the question.

Sec. 14. The board of supervisors of each organized county may organize and consolidate townships under restrictions and limitations provided by law.

Sec. 15. Any county, when authorized by its board of supervisors shall have the authority to enter or to intervene in any action or certificate proceeding involving the services, charges or rates of any privately owned public utility furnishing services or commodities to rate payers within the county.

Sec. 16. The legislature may provide for the laying out, construction, improvement and maintenance of highways, bridges, culverts and airports by the state and by the counties and townships thereof; and may authorize counties to take charge and control of any highway within their limits for such purposes. The legislature may provide the powers and duties of counties in relation to highways, bridges, culverts and airports; may provide for county road commissioners to be appointed or elected, with powers and duties provided by law. The ad valorem property tax imposed for road purposes by any county shall not exceed in any year one-half of one percent of the assessed valuation for the preceding year.

Sec. 17. Each organized township shall be a body corporate with powers and immunities provided by law.

Sec. 18. In each organized township there shall be elected for terms of not less than two nor more than four years as prescribed by law a supervisor, a clerk, a treasurer, and not to exceed four trustees, whose legislative and administrative powers and duties shall be provided by law.

Sec. 19. No organized township shall grant any public utility franchise which is not subject to revocation at the will of the township, unless the proposition shall first have been approved by a majority of the electors of such township voting thereon at a regular or special election.

Sec. 20. The legislature shall provide by law for the dissolution of township government whenever all the territory of an organized township is included within the boundaries of a village or villages notwithstanding that a village may include territory within another organized township and provide by law for the classification of such village or villages as cities.

Sec. 21. The legislature shall provide by general laws for the incorporation of cities and villages. Such laws shall limit their rate of ad valorem property taxation for municipal purposes, and restrict the powers of cities and villages to borrow money and contract debts. Each city and village is granted power to levy other taxes for public purposes, subject to limitations and prohibitions provided by this constitution or by law.

Sec. 22. Under general laws the electors of each city and village shall have the power and authority to frame, adopt and amend its charter, and to amend an existing charter of the city or village heretofore granted or enacted by the legislature for the government of the city or village. Each such city and village shall have power to adopt resolutions and ordinances relating to its municipal concerns, property and government, subject to the constitution and law. No enumeration of powers granted to cities and villages in this constitution shall limit or restrict the general grant of authority conferred by this section.

Sec. 23. Any city or village may acquire, own, establish and maintain, within or without its corporate limits, parks, boulevards, cemeteries, hospitals and all works which involve the public health or safety.

Sec. 24. Subject to this constitution, any city or village may acquire, own or operate, within or without its corporate limits, public service facilities for supplying water, light, heat, power, sewage disposal and transportation to the municipality and the inhabitants thereof.

Any city or village may sell and deliver heat, power or light without its corporate limits in an amount not exceeding 25 percent of that furnished by it within the corporate limits, except as greater amounts may be permitted by law; may sell and deliver water and provide sewage disposal services outside of its corporate limits in such amount as may be determined by the legislative body of the city or village; and may operate transportation lines outside the municipality within such limits as may be prescribed by law.

Sec. 25. No city or village shall acquire any public utility furnishing light, heat or power, or grant any public utility franchise which is not subject to revocation at the will of the city or village, unless the proposition shall first have been approved by three-fifths of the electors voting thereon. No city or village may sell any public utility unless the proposition shall first have been approved by a majority of the electors voting thereon, or a greater number if the charter shall so provide.

Sec. 26. Except as otherwise provided in this constitution, no city or village shall have the power to loan its credit for any private purpose or, except as provided by law, for any public purpose.

Sec. 27. Notwithstanding any other provision of this constitution the legislature may establish in metropolitan areas additional forms of government or authorities with powers, duties and jurisdictions as the legislature shall provide. Wherever possible, such additional forms of government or authorities shall be designed to perform multi-purpose functions rather than a single function.

Sec. 28. The legislature by general law shall authorize two or more counties, townships, cities, villages or districts, or any combination thereof among other things to:

enter into contractual undertakings or agreements with one another or with the state or with any combination thereof for the joint administration of any of the functions or powers which each would have the power to perform separately; share the costs and responsibilities of functions and services with one another or with the state or with any combination thereof which each would have the power to perform separately; transfer functions or responsibilities to one another or any combination thereof upon the consent of each unit involved; cooperate with one another and with state government; lend their credit to one another or any combination thereof as provided by law in connection with any authorized publicly owned undertaking.

Any other provision of this constitution notwithstanding, an officer or employee of the state or any such unit of government or subdivision or agency thereof, except members of the legislature, may serve on or with any governmental body established for the purposes set forth in this section and shall not be required to relinquish his office or employment by reason of such service.

Sec. 29. No person, partnership, association or corporation, public or private, operating a public utility shall have the right to the use of the highways, streets, alleys or other public places of any county, township, city or village for wires, poles, pipes, tracks, conduits or other utility facilities, without the consent of the duly constituted authority of the county, township, city or village; or to transact local business therein without first obtaining a franchise from the township, city or village. Except as otherwise provided in this constitution the right of all counties, townships, cities and villages to the reasonable control of their highways, streets, alleys and public places is hereby reserved to such local units of government.

Sec. 30. No franchise or license shall be granted by any township, city or village for a period longer than 30 years.

Sec. 31. The legislature shall not vacate or alter any road, street, alley or public place under the jurisdiction of any county, township, city or village.

Sec. 32. Any county, township, city, village, authority or school district empowered by the legislature or by this constitution to prepare budgets of estimated expenditures and revenues shall adopt such budgets only after a public hearing in a manner prescribed by law.

Sec. 33. Any elected officer of a political subdivision may be removed from office in the manner and for the causes provided by law.

Sec. 34. The provisions of this constitution and law concerning counties, townships, cities and villages shall be liberally construed in their favor. Powers granted to counties and townships by this constitution and by law shall include those fairly implied and not prohibited by this constitution.

ARTICLE VIII

Education

Sec. 1. Religion, morality and knowledge being necessary to good government and the happiness of mankind, schools and the means of education shall forever be encouraged.

Sec. 2. The legislature shall maintain and support a system of free public elementary and secondary schools as defined by law. Every school district shall provide for the education of its pupils without discrimination as to religion, creed, race, color or national origin.

Sec. 3. Leadership and general supervision over all public education, including adult education and instructional programs in state institutions, except as to institutions of higher education granting baccalaureate degrees, is vested in a state board of education. It shall serve as the general planning and coordinating body for all public education, including higher education, and shall advise the legislature as to the financial requirements in connection therewith.

The state board of education shall appoint a superintendent of public instruction whose term of office shall be determined by the board. He shall be the chairman of the board without the right to vote, and shall be responsible for the execution of its policies. He shall be the principal executive officer of a state department of education which shall have powers and duties provided by law.

The state board of education shall consist of eight members who shall be nominated by party conventions and elected at large for terms of eight years as prescribed by law. The governor shall fill any vacancy by appointment for the unexpired term. The governor shall be ex-officio a member of the state board of education without the right to vote.

The power of the boards of institutions of higher education provided in this constitution to supervise their respective institutions and control and direct the expenditure of the institutions' funds shall not be limited by this section.

Sec. 4. The legislature shall appropriate moneys to maintain the University of Michigan, Michigan State University, Wayne State University, Eastern Michigan University, Michigan College of Science and Technology, Central Michigan University, Northern Michigan University, Western Michigan University, Ferris Institute, Grand Valley State College, by whatever names such institutions may hereafter be known, and other institutions of higher education established by law. The legislature shall be given an annual accounting of all income and expenditures by each of these educational institutions. Formal sessions of governing boards of such institutions shall be open to the public.

Sec. 5. The regents of the University of Michigan and their successors in office shall constitute a body corporate known as the Regents of the University of Michigan; the trustees of Michigan State University and their successors in office shall constitute a body corporate known as the Board of Trustees of Michigan State University; the governors of Wayne State University and their successors in office shall constitute a body corporate known as the Board of Governors of Wayne State University. Each board shall have general supervision of its institution and the control and direction of all expenditures from the institution's funds. Each board shall, as often as necessary, elect a president of the institution under its supervision. He shall be the principal executive officer of the institution, be ex-officio a member of the board without the right to vote and preside at meetings of the board. The board of each institution shall consist of eight members who shall hold office for terms of eight years and who shall be elected as provided by law. The governor shall fill board vacancies by appointment. Each appointee shall hold office until a successor has been nominated and elected as provided by law.

Sec. 6. Other institutions of higher education established by law having authority to grant baccalaureate degrees shall each be governed by a board of control which shall be a body corporate. The board shall have general supervision of the institution and the control and direction of all expenditures from the institution's funds. It shall, as often as necessary, elect a president of the institution under its supervision.

He shall be the principal executive officer of the institution and be ex-officio a member of the board without the right to vote. The board may elect one of its members or may designate the president, to preside at board meetings. Each board of control shall consist of eight members who shall hold office for terms of eight years, not more than two of which shall expire in the same year, and who shall be appointed by the governor by and with the advice and consent of the senate. Vacancies shall be filled in like manner.

Sec. 7. The legislature shall provide by law for the establishment and financial support of public community and junior colleges which shall be supervised and controlled by locally elected boards. The legislature shall provide by law for a state board for public community and junior colleges which shall advise the state board of education concerning general supervision and planning for such colleges and requests for annual appropriations for their support. The board shall consist of eight members who shall hold office for terms of eight years, not more than two of which shall expire in the same year, and who shall be appointed by the state board of education. Vacancies shall be filled in like manner. The superintendent of public instruction shall be ex-officio a member of this board without the right to vote.

Sec. 8. Institutions, programs and services for the care, treatment, education or rehabilitation of those inhabitants who are physically, mentally or otherwise seriously handicapped shall always be fostered and supported.

Sec. 9. The legislature shall provide by law for the establishment and support of public libraries which shall be available to all residents of the state under regulations adopted by the governing bodies thereof. All fines assessed and collected in the several counties, townships and cities for any breach of the penal laws shall be exclusively applied to the support of such public libraries, and county law libraries as provided by law.

ARTICLE IX

Finance and Taxation

Sec. 1. The legislature shall impose taxes sufficient with other resources to pay the expenses of state government.

Sec. 2. The power of taxation shall never be surrendered, suspended or contracted away.

Sec. 3. The legislature shall provide for the uniform general ad valorem taxation of real and tangible personal property not exempt by law. The legislature shall provide for the determination of true cash value of such property; the proportion of true cash value at which such property shall be uniformly assessed, which shall not, after January 1, 1966, exceed 50 percent; and for a system of equalization of assessments. The legislature may provide for alternative means of taxation of designated real and tangible personal property in lieu of general ad valorem taxation. Every tax other than the general ad valorem property tax shall be uniform upon the class or classes on which it operates.

Sec. 4. Property owned and occupied by non-profit religious or educational organizations and used exclusively for religious or educational purposes, as defined by law, shall be exempt from real and personal property taxes.

Sec. 5. The legislature shall provide for the assessment by the state of the property of those public service businesses assessed by the state at the date this constitution becomes effective, and of other property as designated by the legislature, and for the imposition and collection of taxes thereon. Property assessed by the state shall be assessed at the same proportion of its true cash value as the legislature shall specify for property subject to general ad valorem taxation. The rate of taxation on such property shall be the average rate levied upon other property in this state under the general ad valorem tax law, or, if the legislature provides, the rate of tax applicable to the property of each business enterprise assessed by the state shall be the average rate of ad valorem taxation levied upon other property in all counties in which any of such property is situated.

Sec. 6. Except as otherwise provided in this constitution, the total amount of general ad valorem taxes imposed upon real and tangible personal property for all purposes in any one year shall not exceed 15 mills on each dollar of the assessed valuation of property as finally equalized. Under procedures provided by law, which shall guarantee the right of initiative, separate tax limitations for any county and for the townships and for school districts therein, the aggregate of which shall not exceed 18 mills on each dollar of such valuation, may be adopted and thereafter altered by the vote of a majority of the qualified electors of such county voting thereon, in lieu of the limitation hereinbefore established. These limitations may be increased to an aggregate of not to exceed 50 mills on each dollar of valuation, for a period of not to exceed 20 years at any one time, if approved by a majority of the electors, qualified under Section 6 of Article II of this constitution, voting on the question.

The foregoing limitations shall not apply to taxes imposed for the payment of principal and interest on bonds or other evidences of indebtedness or for the payment of assessments or contract obligations in anticipation of which bonds are issued, which taxes may be imposed without limitation as to rate or amount; or to taxes imposed for any other purpose by any city, village, charter county, charter township, charter authority or other authority, the tax limitations of which are provided by charter or by general law.

In any school district which extends into two or more counties, property taxes at the highest rate available in the county which contains the greatest part of the area of the district may be imposed and collected for school purposes throughout the district.

Sec. 7. No income tax graduated as to rate or base shall be imposed by the state or any of its subdivisions.

Sec. 8. The legislature shall not impose a sales tax on retailers at a rate of more than four percent of their gross taxable sales of tangible personal property.

Sec. 9. All specific taxes, except general sales and use taxes and regulatory fees, imposed directly or indirectly on fuels sold or used to propel motor vehicles upon highways and on registered motor vehicles shall, after the payment of necessary collection expenses, be used exclusively for highway purposes as defined by law.

Sec. 10. One-eighth of all taxes imposed on retailers on taxable sales at retail of tangible personal property shall be used exclusively for assistance to townships, cities and villages, on a population basis as provided by law. In determining population the legislature may exclude any portion of the total number of persons who are wards, patients or convicts in any tax supported institution.

Sec. 11. There shall be established a state school aid fund which shall be used exclusively for aid to school districts, higher education and school employees' retirement systems, as provided by law. One-half of all taxes imposed on retailers on taxable sales at retail of tangible personal property, and other tax revenues provided by law, shall be dedicated to this fund. Payments from this fund shall be made in full on a scheduled basis, as provided by law.

Sec. 12. No evidence of state indebtedness shall be issued except for debts authorized pursuant to this constitution.

Sec. 13. Public bodies corporate shall have power to borrow money and to issue their securities evidencing debt, subject to this constitution and law.

Sec. 14. To meet obligations incurred pursuant to appropriations for any fiscal year, the legislature may by law authorize the state to issue its full faith and credit notes in which case it shall pledge undedicated revenues to be received within the same fiscal year for the repayment thereof. Such indebtedness in any fiscal year shall not exceed 15 percent of undedicated revenues received by the state during the preceding fiscal year and such debts shall be repaid at the time the revenues so pledged are received, but not later than the end of the same fiscal year.

Sec. 15. The state may borrow money for specific purposes in amounts as may be provided by acts of the legislature adopted by a vote of two-thirds of the members elected to and serving in each house, and approved by a majority of the electors voting thereon at any general election. The question submitted to the electors shall state the amount to be borrowed, the specific purpose to which the funds shall be devoted, and the method of repayment.

Sec. 16. The state, in addition to any other borrowing power, may borrow from time to time such amounts as shall be required, pledge its faith and credit and issue its notes or bonds therefor, for the purpose of making loans to school districts as provided in this section.

If the minimum amount which would otherwise be necessary for a school district to levy in any year to pay principal and interest on its qualified bonds, including any necessary allowances for estimated tax delinquencies, exceeds 13 mills on each dollar of its assessed valuation as finally equalized, or such lower millage as the legislature may prescribe, then the school district may elect to borrow all or any part of the excess from the state. In that event the state shall lend the excess amount to the school district for the payment of principal and interest. If for any reason any school district will be or is unable to pay the principal and interest on its qualified bonds when due, then the school district shall borrow and the state shall lend to it an amount sufficient to enable the school district to make the payment.

The term "qualified bonds" means general obligation bonds of school districts issued for capital expenditures, including refunding bonds, issued prior to May 4, 1955, or issued thereafter and qualified as provided by law pursuant to Section 27 or Section 28 of Article X of the Constitution of 1908 or pursuant to this section.

After a school district has received loans from the state, each year thereafter it shall levy for debt service, exclusive of levies for nonqualified bonds, not less than 13 mills or such lower millage as the legislature may prescribe, until the amount loaned has been repaid, and any tax collections therefrom in any year over and above the minimum requirements for principal and interest on qualified bonds shall be used toward the repayment of state loans. In any year when such levy would produce an amount in excess of the requirements and the amount due to the state, the levy may be reduced by the amount of the excess.

Subject to the foregoing provisions, the legislature shall have the power to prescribe and to limit the procedure, terms and conditions for the qualification of bonds, for obtaining and making state loans, and for the repayment of loans.

The power to tax for the payment of principal and interest on bonds hereafter issued which are the general obligations of any school district, including refunding bonds, and for repayment of any state loans made to school districts, shall be without limitation as to rate or amount.

All rights acquired under Sections 27 and 28 of Article X of the Constitution of 1908, by holders of bonds heretofore issued, and all obligations assumed by the state or any school district under these sections, shall remain unimpaired.

Sec. 17. No money shall be paid out of the state treasury except in pursuance of appropriations made by law.

Sec. 18. The credit of the state shall not be granted to, nor in aid of any person, association or corporation, public or private, except as authorized in this constitution.

This section shall not be construed to prohibit the investment of public funds until needed for current requirements or the investment of funds accumulated to provide retirement or pension benefits for public officials and employees, as provided by law.

Sec. 19. The state shall not subscribe to, nor be interested in the stock of any company, association or corporation, except that funds accumulated to provide retirement or pension benefits for public officials and employees may be invested as provided by law; and endowment funds created for charitable or educational purposes may be invested as provided by law governing the investment of funds held in trust by trustees.

Sec. 20. No state money shall be deposited in banks other than those organized under the national or state banking laws. No state money shall be deposited in any bank in excess of 50 percent of the capital and surplus of such bank. Any bank receiving deposits of state money shall show the amount of state money so deposited as a separate item in all published statements.

Sec. 21. The legislature shall provide by law for the annual accounting for all public moneys, state and local, and may provide by law for interim accounting.

The legislature shall provide by law for the maintenance of uniform accounting systems by units of local government and the auditing of county accounts by competent state authority and other units of government as provided by law.

Sec. 22. Procedures for the examination and adjustment of claims against the state shall be prescribed by law.

Sec. 23. All financial records, accountings, audit reports and other reports of public moneys shall be public records and open to inspection. A statement of all revenues and expenditures of public moneys shall be published and distributed annually, as provided by law.

Sec. 24. The accrued financial benefits of each pension plan and retirement system of the state and its political subdivisions shall be a contractual obligation thereof which shall not be diminished or impaired thereby.

Financial benefits arising on account of service rendered in each fiscal year shall be funded during that year and such funding shall not be used for financing unfunded accrued liabilities.

ARTICLE X
Property

Sec. 1. The disabilities of coverture as to property are abolished. The real and personal estate of every woman acquired before marriage and all real and personal property to which she may afterwards become entitled shall be and remain the estate and property of such woman, and shall not be liable for the debts, obligations or engagements of her husband, and may be dealt with and disposed of by her as if she were unmarried. Dower may be relinquished or conveyed as provided by law.

Sec. 2. Private property shall not be taken for public use without just compensation therefor being first made or secured in a manner prescribed by law. Compensation shall be determined in proceedings in a court of record.

Sec. 3. A homestead in the amount of not less than $3,500 and personal property of every resident of this state in the amount of not less than $750, as defined by law, shall be exempt from forced sale on execution or other process of any court. Such exemptions shall not extend to any lien thereon excluded from exemption by law.

Sec. 4. Procedures relating to escheats and to the custody and disposition of escheated property shall be prescribed by law.

Sec. 5. The legislature shall have general supervisory jurisdiction over all state owned lands useful for forest preserves, game areas and recreational purposes; shall require annual reports as to such lands from all departments having supervision or control thereof; and shall by general law provide for the sale, lease or other disposition of such lands.

The legislature by an act adopted by two-thirds of the members elected to and serving in each house may designate any part of such lands as a state land reserve. No lands in the state land reserve may be removed from the reserve, sold, leased or otherwise disposed of except by an act of the legislature.

Sec. 6. Aliens who are residents of this state shall enjoy the same rights and privileges in property as citizens of this state.

ARTICLE XI

Public Officers and Employment

Sec. 1. All officers, legislative, executive and judicial, before entering upon the duties of their respective offices, shall take and subscribe the following oath or affirmation: I do solemnly swear (or affirm) that I will support the Constitution of the United States and the constitution of this state, and that I will faithfully discharge the duties of the office of .... according to the best of my ability. No other oath, affirmation, or any religious test shall be required as a qualification for any office or public trust.

Sec. 2. The terms of office of elective state officers, members of the legislature and justices and judges of courts of record shall begin at twelve o'clock noon on the first day of January next succeeding their election, except as otherwise provided in this constitution. The terms of office of county officers shall begin on the first day of January next succeeding their election, except as otherwise provided by law.

Sec. 3. Neither the legislature nor any political subdivision of this state shall grant or authorize extra compensation to any public officer, agent or contractor after the service has been rendered or the contract entered into.

Sec. 4. No person having custody or control of public moneys shall be a member of the legislature, or be eligible to any office of trust or profit under this state, until he shall have made an accounting, as provided by law, of all sums for which he may be liable.

Sec. 5. The classified state civil service shall consist of all positions in the state service except those filled by popular election, heads of principal departments, members of boards and commissions, the principal executive officer of boards and commissions heading principal departments, employees of courts of record, employees of the legislature, employees of the state institutions of higher education, all persons in the armed forces of the state, eight exempt positions in the office of the governor, and within each principal department, when requested by the department head, two other exempt positions, one of which shall be policy-making. The civil service commission may exempt three additional positions of a policy-making nature within each principal department.

The civil service commission shall be non-salaried and shall consist of four persons, not more than two of whom shall be members of the same political party, appointed by the governor for terms of eight years, no two of which shall expire in the same year.

The administration of the commission's powers shall be vested in a state personnel director who shall be a member of the classified service and who shall be responsible to and selected by the commission after open competitive examination.

The commission shall classify all positions in the classified service according to their respective duties and responsibilities, fix rates of compensation for all classes of positions, approve or disapprove disbursements for all personal services, determine by competitive examination and performance exclusively on the basis of merit, efficiency and fitness the qualifications of all candidates for positions in the classified service, make rules and regulations covering all personnel transactions, and regulate all conditions of employment in the classified service.

No person shall be appointed to or promoted in the classified service who has not been certified by the commission as qualified for such appointment or promotion. No appointments, promotions, demotions or removals in the classified service shall be made for religious, racial or partisan considerations.

Increases in rates of compensation authorized by the commission may be effective only at the start of a fiscal year and shall require prior notice to the governor, who shall transmit such increases to the legislature as part of his budget. The legislature may, by a majority vote of the members elected to and serving in each house, waive the notice and permit increases in rates of compensation to be effective at a time other than the start of a fiscal year. Within 60 calendar days following such transmission, the legislature may, by a two-thirds vote of the members elected to and serving in each house, reject or reduce increases in rates of compensation authorized by the commission. Any reduction ordered by the legislature shall apply uniformly to all classes of employees affected by the increases and shall not adjust pay differentials already established by the civil service commission. The legislature may not reduce rates of compensation below those in effect at the time of the transmission of increases authorized by the commission.

The appointing authorities may create or abolish positions for reasons of administrative efficiency without the approval of the commission. Positions shall not be created nor abolished except for reasons of administrative efficiency. Any employee considering himself aggrieved by the abolition or creation of a position shall have a right of appeal to the commission through established grievance procedures.

The civil service commission shall recommend to the governor and to the legislature rates of compensation for all appointed positions within the executive department not a part of the classified service.

To enable the commission to exercise its powers, the legislature shall appropriate to the commission for the ensuing fiscal year a sum not less than one percent of the aggregate payroll of the classified service for the preceding fiscal year, as certified by the commission. Within six months after the conclusion of each fiscal year the commission shall return to the state treasury all moneys unexpended for that fiscal year.

The commission shall furnish reports of expenditures, at least annually, to the governor and the legislature and shall be subject to annual audit as provided by law.

No payment for personal services shall be made or authorized until the provisions of this constitution pertaining to civil service have been complied with in every particular. Violation of any of the provisions hereof may be restrained or observance compelled by injunctive or mandamus proceedings brought by any citizen of the state.

Sec. 6. By ordinance or resolution of its governing body which shall not take effect until approved by a majority of the electors voting thereon, unless otherwise provided by charter, each county, township, city, village, school district and other governmental unit or authority may establish, modify or discontinue a merit system for its employees other than teachers under contract or tenure. The state civil service commission may on request furnish technical services to any such unit on a reimbursable basis.

Sec. 7. The house of representatives shall have the sole power of impeaching civil officers for corrupt conduct in office or for crimes or misdemeanors, but a majority of the members elected thereto and serving therein shall be necessary to direct an impeachment.

When an impeachment is directed, the house of representatives shall elect three of its members to prosecute the impeachment.

Every impeachment shall be tried by the senate immediately after the final adjournment of the legislature. The senators shall take an oath or affirmation truly and impartially to try and determine the impeachment according to the evidence. When the governor or lieutenant governor is tried, the chief justice of the supreme court shall preside.

No person shall be convicted without the concurrence of two-thirds of the senators elected and serving. Judgment in case of conviction shall not extend further than removal from office, but the person convicted shall be liable to punishment according to law.

No judicial officer shall exercise any of the functions of his office after an impeachment is directed until he is acquitted.

ARTICLE XII

Amendment and Revision

Sec. 1. Amendments to this constitution may be proposed in the senate or house of representatives. Proposed amendments agreed to by two-thirds of the members elected to and serving in each house on a vote with the names and vote of those voting entered in the respective journals shall be submitted, not less than 60 days thereafter, to the electors at the next general election or special election as the legislature shall direct. If a majority of electors voting on a proposed amendment approve the same, it shall become part of the constitution and shall abrogate or amend existing provisions of the constitution at the end of 45 days after the date of the election at which it was approved.

Sec. 2. Amendments may be proposed to this constitution by petition of the registered electors of this state. Every petition shall include the full text of the proposed amendment, and be signed by registered electors of the state equal in number to at least 10 percent of the total vote cast for all candidates for governor at the last preceding general election at which a governor was elected. Such petitions shall be filed with the person authorized by law to receive the same at least 120 days before the election at which the proposed amendment is to be voted upon. Any such petition shall be in the form, and shall be signed and circulated in such manner, as prescribed by law. The person authorized by law to receive such petition shall upon its receipt determine, as provided by law, the validity and sufficiency of the signatures on the petition, and make an official announcement thereof at least 60 days prior to the election at which the proposed amendment is to be voted upon.

Any amendment proposed by such petition shall be submitted, not less than 120 days after it was filed, to the electors at the next general election. Such proposed amendment, existing provisions of the constitution which would be altered or abrogated thereby, and the question as it shall appear on the ballot shall be published in full as provided by law. Copies of such publication shall be posted in each polling place and furnished to news media as provided by law.

The ballot to be used in such election shall contain a statement of the purpose of the proposed amendment, expressed in not more than 100 words, exclusive of caption. Such statement of purpose and caption shall be prepared by the person authorized by law, and shall consist of a true and impartial statement of the purpose of the amendment in such language as shall create no prejudice for or against the proposed amendment.

If the proposed amendment is approved by a majority of the electors voting on the question, it shall become part of the constitution, and shall abrogate or amend existing provisions of the constitution at the end of 45 days after the date of the election at which it was approved. If two or more amendments approved by the electors at the same election conflict, that amendment receiving the highest affirmative vote shall prevail.

Sec. 3. At the general election to be held in the year 1978, and in each 16th year thereafter and at such times as may be provided by law, the question of a general revision of the constitution shall be submitted to the electors of the state. If a majority of the electors voting on the question decide in favor of a convention for such purpose, at an election to be held not later than six months after the proposal was certified as approved, the electors of each representative district as then organized shall elect one delegate and the electors of each senatorial district as then organized shall elect one delegate at a partisan election. The delegates so elected shall convene at the seat of government on the first Tuesday in October next succeeding such election or at an earlier date if provided by law.

The convention shall choose its own officers, determine the rules of its proceedings and judge the qualifications, elections and returns of its members. To fill a vacancy in the office of any delegate, the governor shall appoint a qualified resident of the same district who shall be a member of the same party as the delegate vacating the office. The convention shall have power to appoint such officers, employees and assistants as it deems necessary and to fix their compensation; to provide for the printing and distribution of its documents, journals and proceedings; to explain and disseminate information about the proposed constitution and to complete the business of the convention in an orderly manner. Each delegate shall receive for his services compensation provided by law.

No proposed constitution or amendment adopted by such convention shall be submitted to the electors for approval as hereinafter provided unless by the assent of a majority of all the delegates elected to and serving in the convention, with the names and vote of those voting entered in the journal. Any proposed constitution or amendments adopted by such convention shall be submitted to the qualified electors in the manner and at the time provided by such convention not less than 90 days after final adjournment of the convention. Upon the approval of such constitution or amendments by a majority of the qualified electors voting thereon the constitution or amendments shall take effect as provided by the convention.

Schedule and Temporary Provisions

To insure the orderly transition from the constitution of 1908 to this constitution the following schedule and temporary provisions are set forth to be effective for such period as are thereby required.

Sec. 1. The attorney general shall recommend to the legislature as soon as practicable such changes as may be necessary to adapt existing laws to this constitution.

Sec. 2. All writs, actions, suits, proceedings, civil or criminal liabilities, prosecutions, judgments, sentences, orders, decrees, appeals, causes of action, contracts, claims, demands, titles and rights existing on the effective date of this constitution shall continue unaffected except as modified in accordance with the provisions of this constitution.

Sec. 3. Except as otherwise provided in this constitution, all officers filling any office by election or appointment shall continue to exercise their powers and duties until their offices shall have been abolished or their successors selected and qualified in accordance with this constitution or the laws enacted pursuant thereto.

No provision of this constitution, or of law or of executive order authorized by this constitution shall shorten the term of any person elected to state office at a statewide election on or prior to the date on which this constitution is submitted to a vote. In the event the duties of any such officers shall not have been abolished or incorporated into one or more of the principal departments at the expiration of his term, such officer shall continue to serve until his duties are so incorporated or abolished.

Sec. 4. All officers elected at the same election that this constitution is submitted to the people for adoption shall take office and complete the term to which they were elected under the 1908 constitution and existing laws and continue to serve until their successors are elected and qualified pursuant to this constitution or law.

Sec. 5. Notwithstanding any other provision in this constitution, the governor, the lieutenant governor, the secretary of state, the attorney general and state senators shall be elected at the general election in 1964 to serve for two-year terms beginning on the first day of January next succeeding their election. The first election of such officers for four-year terms under this constitution shall be held at the general election in 1966.

Sec. 6. Notwithstanding the provisions of this constitution that the supreme court shall consist of seven justices it shall consist of eight justices until the time that a vacancy occurs as a result of death, retirement or resignation of a justice. The first such vacancy shall not be filled.

Sec. 7. Any judge of probate serving on the effective date of this constitution may serve the remainder of the term and be eligible to succeed himself for election regardless of other provisions in this constitution requiring him to be licensed to practice law in this state.

Sec. 8. The provisions of Article VI providing that terms of judicial offices shall not all expire at the same time, shall be implemented by law providing that at the next election for such offices judges shall be elected for terms of varying length, none of which shall be shorter than the regular term provided for the office.

Sec. 9. The members of the state board of education provided for in Section 3 of Article VIII of this constitution shall first be elected at the first general election after the effective date of this constitution for the following terms: two shall be elected for two years, two for four years, two for six years, and two for eight years as prescribed by law.

The state board of education provided for in the constitution of 1908 is abolished at twelve o'clock noon January 1 of the year following the first general election under this constitution and the terms of members thereof shall then expire.

Sec. 10. The provisions of this constitution providing for members of boards of control of institutions of higher education and the state board of public community and junior colleges shall be implemented by law. The law may provide that the term of each member in office on the date of the vote on this constitution may be extended, and may further provide that the initial terms of office of members may be less than eight years.

Sec. 11. The provisions of this constitution increasing the number of members of the Board of Trustees of Michigan State University and of the Board of Governors of Wayne State University to eight, and of their term of office to eight years, shall be implemented by law. The law may provide that the term of each member in office on the date of the vote on this constitution may be extended one year, and may further provide that the initial terms of office of the additional members may be less than eight years.

Sec. 12. The initial allocation of departments by law pursuant to Section 2 of Article V of this constitution, shall be completed within two years after the effective date of this constitution. If such allocation shall not have been completed within such period, the governor, within one year thereafter, by executive order, shall make the initial allocation.

Sec. 13. Contractual obligations of the state incurred pursuant to the constitution of 1908 shall continue to be obligations of the state.

For the retirement of notes and bonds issued under Section 26 of Article X of the 1908 constitution, there is hereby appropriated from the general fund each year during their life a sum equal to the amount of principal and interest payments due and payable in each year.

Sec. 14. The legislature by a vote of two-thirds of the members elected to and serving in each house may provide that the state may borrow money and may pledge its full faith and credit for refunding any bonds issued by the Mackinac Bridge Authority and at the time of refunding the Mackinac Bridge Authority shall be abolished and the operation of the bridge shall be assumed by the state highway department. The legislature may implement this section by law.

Sec. 15. This constitution shall be submitted to the people for their adoption or rejection at the general election to be held on the first Monday in April, 1963. It shall be the duty of the secretary of state forthwith to give notice of such submission to all other officers required to give or publish any notice in regard to a general election. He shall give notice that this constitution will be duly submitted to the electors at such election. The notice shall be given in the manner required for the election of governor.

Sec. 16. Every registered elector may vote on the adoption of the constitution. The board of election commissioners in each county shall cause to be printed on a ballot separate from the ballot containing the names of the nominees for office, the words: Shall the revised constitution be adopted? ( ) Yes. ( ) No. All votes cast at the election shall be taken, counted, canvassed and returned as provided by law for the election of state officers. If the revised constitution so submitted receives more votes in its favor than were cast against it, it shall be the supreme law of the state on and after the first day of January of the year following its adoption.

Adopted by the Constitutional Convention of nineteen hundred sixty-one at Constitution Hall in Lansing on the first day of August, nineteen hundred sixty-two.

Stephen S. Nisbet

Stephen S. Nisbet, *President*

Fred I. Chase

Fred I. Chase, *Secretary*

Carr, Robert W
Government in Michigan under the 1964 Constitution.